Thomas George Bonney

Old Truths in Modern Lights

The Boyle lectures for 1890 with other sermons

Thomas George Bonney

Old Truths in Modern Lights
The Boyle lectures for 1890 with other sermons

ISBN/EAN: 9783337087623

Printed in Europe, USA, Canada, Australia, Japan

Cover: Foto ©Lupo / pixelio.de

More available books at **www.hansebooks.com**

OLD TRUTHS
IN MODERN LIGHTS

OLD TRUTHS
IN
MODERN LIGHTS

THE BOYLE LECTURES FOR 1890

WITH OTHER SERMONS

BY

T. G. BONNEY, D.Sc.
LL.D., F.R.S., F.S.A., F.G.S.

FELLOW OF ST. JOHN'S COLLEGE, CAMBRIDGE, HONORARY CANON OF MANCHESTER
AND EXAMINING CHAPLAIN TO THE LORD BISHOP OF MANCHESTER

London
PERCIVAL AND CO.
1891

TO MY MOTHER,

WHO, BY HER UNFAILING LOVE,

HAS ENCOURAGED ME TO LABOUR,

BY HER PATIENCE IN SUFFERING HAS BEEN A LIVING LESSON

IN THE WAY OF THE CROSS,

I DEDICATE THIS LITTLE BOOK.

Preface

NOTWITHSTANDING the well-known proverb about making excuses, I must venture to apologize for an obvious defect in the present book. The discourses contained in it were written at different times, without any idea that they would emerge from the stage of manuscript. On being requested to publish a volume of sermons, I selected for this purpose those which appeared to me to have more relation than others to questions which at the present day often exercise, and sometimes disturb, the minds of thoughtful Christians. Thus, occasionally, I have had to choose between repeating myself, and destroying the coherence of a sermon by making excisions; and, on the whole, I have preferred the former course. In one case, indeed, the repetition has been deliberate; for the final discourse in this volume deals with a subject which has been more than glanced at in one of the Boyle Lectures. But as I think the matter one of considerable interest, and do not remember to have read any discussion of it from quite the same point of view, I have ventured to hope that a more full treatment than was permitted by the limits of those lectures might be of interest to some readers.

I wish also to state that if any resemblances be observed between passages in this book and the well-known work entitled *Lux Mundi*, they are fortuitous. As the dates appended will show, most of these sermons, except the Boyle Lectures, were written before that work was published.[1] As it happened, when I was asked, unavoidably at rather short notice, to undertake to give those lectures, I had been so much engaged as to be unable to find time to read *Lux Mundi*. Hence, as I was even then greatly pressed by my ordinary duties, I thought it best to follow my usual plan in like circumstances,

---

[1] Six of them were preached at St. Peter's, Vere Street, in 1889, when the Rev. W. Page Roberts was absent for three months owing to a serious illness.

Three of the sermons in this volume have been published in the *Church of England Pulpit*, and I am indebted to the courtesy of the Editor for permission to reprint them.

namely, to confine my reading to books which would be more likely to impugn than to maintain my own views.

Lux Mundi marks, in my opinion, an important epoch in the history of religious thought in the present century. It is, in a certain sense, a prognostic of a coming reformation, and can hardly fail to produce effects more far-reaching than perhaps its authors either foresaw or have even yet foreseen. Common report reckons them in the ranks of what is usually called the High Church party. In their book the necessity of applying scientific principles to the treatment of theological questions is virtually admitted. This concession will be found, I think, either to place them in an extremely unstable position between the conflicting claims of reason and authority, or to force them irresistibly to abandon much which has hitherto been regarded by their own party as of primary importance. They have given up, so to say, a position which was the key of their defence, and its abandonment will render untenable a rather imposing line of outworks. This probably has been perceived by some of the more keen-sighted among the High Church party, and has been the real cause of the vehement indignation which the book has aroused in certain quarters.

It is quite true—and on this matter we should be agreed—that no small part of the faith held in common by Christians of various denominations cannot be assailed by methods strictly scientific, and is perfectly compatible with scientific progress. The spiritual order is one thing, the physical order is another; though there may be occasionally common ground between them, and special difficulties may result as a consequence.

But there are also certain doctrines which, generally speaking, are characteristic only of particular branches of the Church, or of particular aggregates of Christians, with which Science can make no truce, and to which she will show no quarter.

Some of these have become exceptionally prominent of late years. During the present century two great religious movements have been witnessed, and we are now feeling more than the premonitory tremors of a third. The first of these, indeed, began in the eighteenth century, but its effects were more generally conspicuous early in the present one. I refer, of course, to the great "Evangelical" movement, which produced a stirring in the "dry bones" of Hanoverian Churchmanship, the blessings of which can hardly be overrated. It brought into strong relief the principle of "individualism" in religion; but, as is the case in politics, this had its own dangers and defects. Its system of theology was narrow and inexpansive; it sometimes came dangerously near to being tainted with Manichean error; it insisted upon regarding nature and the world from a single standpoint, and thus, as a rule, dissociated itself from learning, culture, and many healthful influences. It also overlooked the importance of historic continuity and the value of corporate action, sentiment, and influences.

These defects brought in a speedy decadence among its leaders; these, of late years, have caused its many excellences to be overlooked and forgotten. Then came the great "Catholic" reaction, which was called at first the Oxford movement. Its upholders were strong exactly where their predecessors were weak. Men found there was a place in religion for learning, for art, and for poetry; that the Church of the nineteenth century claimed to be in organic connection with that not only of the first, but also of all succeeding centuries, and was in possession of a literature which was a rich mine of noble thoughts and devout aspirations. The learning, the ability, and the personal holiness of some of its earliest leaders contributed much to the success of this movement, which stood in some respects in the same relation to the former (though obviously the comparison cannot be pressed far) as does socialism to individualism. Doubtless, also, some of its success is due to the attractions which it offers to sundry obvious weaknesses in human nature. What wonder if a young man recently ordained should feel the fascination of "high views" as to sacerdotal authority, when he is fully conscious that only a few months since no one cared much about his opinion on any question of importance! What wonder if those Christians—a rather numerous group—who are afraid, like some young children, to walk without the supporting hand of a nurse, should surrender themselves willingly to the guidance of a "spiritual director"! So this movement has had its day of triumph, which has surprised those who had confidence in the sturdy independence and strong common sense of the Englishman. But now a habit is growing up, hitherto not so much within as without the clerical order, a habit induced by the vast progress which has been made in scientific investigation and by the consequent methods of thought and reasoning, of looking at every question from the standpoint of an unfettered inquirer. The dominant school is content with authorities, the new one requires facts; the one is literary, the other scientific in its methods; the one, like a lawyer, seeks for precedents and for decrees; the other, for reasons and for principles. Tell the former that a certain good man, who died a thousand years ago, held such and such an opinion, and as a rule he is satisfied; tell the same to the latter, and he remarks that the fact is interesting in its bearing on the history of thought, but inquires whether the people of that age had better means of coming to a decision, or indeed so good, as are possessed by those of the present.

This new spirit, before long, cannot fail to come into sharp conflict with that which at the present day commands a large number, possibly, at any rate among the clergy of the Church of England, even a majority, of adherents, who are eagerly contending for and insisting on the primary importance of those doctrines and those methods of worship which arrogate to themselves the title of Catholic. In regard to those doctrines and practices, especially the latter, many zealous advocates appear to have no clear idea as to their own position. This may be due to the influences to which they have been exposed. But if they fall into scientific habits of thought, the question will be presented to them somewhat in this way: "We are fighting for vestments, candles, and a certain ritual as keenly as if they were almost necessary for salvation. What do we mean by our earnest contention? Do we want these appendages simply to gratify an antiquarian sentiment, or are they really symbolical of doctrine? If the former only, let us disarm opposition by proclaiming their unimportance; and if even then they give serious offence, let us do without them. Surely we are not worse men than our forefathers because we wear a different (and less picturesque) dress! Besides that, there is some reason in the opposition, for these practices in the past undoubtedly proved liable to abuse, and were perverted into superstition. If, however, they are significant of doctrine, at what date did they become important? How far are these things, these ideas, part of the charter of Christianity, as it may be called, or only some of its bye-laws enacted at a time when, as history shows, Christendom was not in a very healthy condition?" For instance, in regard to "eucharistic" and other "vestments," for which some fight strenuously as being symbolical of doctrine; if these vestments prove to be only survivals of the ordinary dress, or of the Sunday clothes (to use a homely phrase), of an epoch three centuries at least after the foundation of Christianity, this symbolism must have been imported into them by a still later age, so that they are only artificially, not really, expressive of doctrine.[1] Again, when we find that some of these

[1] The fact stated above is commonly ignored, and sometimes even denied, by the writers of a certain school, but its truth cannot be disputed by any person who studies antiquities and reads history in a scientific spirit. Of such an investigation the general results will be found in the chapter on "Ecclesiastical Vestments" in the late Dean Stanley's *Christian Institutions*. A more full discussion, with ample materials for study, will be found in the late W. B. Marriott's *Vestiarium Christianum*. He brings forward a mass of evidence, positive

beliefs and claims for perpetual thaumaturgic powers on the part either of individuals or of an order not

and negative, which, as it seems to me, places his conclusions beyond doubt, viz. "that in the Apostolic age there was no essential difference between the dress worn by Christians in ordinary life and that worn by bishops, priests, or other clerics, when engaged in offices of holy ministration; but that, after the lapse of three or four centuries, the dress of ordinary life became changed, while that worn in ecclesiastical offices remained in form unchanged, though ever more and more richly decorated; that from these causes a marked distinction was gradually brought about between the dress of the clergy and that of the laity (to say nothing of the monastic orders, who were distinguished from both); that as time went on the ordinary dress of the clergy themselves came to be distinguished, in form, in colour, and in name, from that in which they ministered, while at length a yet further distinction was introduced between the dress of the more ordinary ministrations and the more splendid vestments reserved for the highest offices of all, and for occasions of especial solemnity" (Introduction, p. ii.).

The remarks above are not intended to refer, even obliquely, to the recent judgment of the Archbishop of Canterbury in the case *Read and Others v. the Lord Bishop of Lincoln* (Nov. 21, 1890). The question before His Grace was one strictly legal—to decide, not whether certain practices were conducive to edification or the reverse, but whether they were contrary to the law of the land. Of that judgment, if I may be permitted to express an opinion, I can only speak in terms of respectful admiration. Personally, I should have been glad if it had been found that more of the practices of which complaint was made were illegal, because they are liable to be perverted to superstition; but after reading the judgment, in which a very intricate question is handled with great learning, with a powerful grasp, and in a spirit truly scientific, it seems clear to me that it will be very difficult to dispute His Grace's decision. The Church, at any rate, gains when it is shown, as in regard to the famous question of the Eastward position, that the practice in dispute has no doctrinal significance at all (pp. 42-45). I could wish the judgment in the case had been accepted. It would have practically extinguished many controversies. One party only cannot be discovered in the charter and title-deeds of the Church, if we read them in a scientific though reverent spirit, but also appear to be repudiated by the writers of these documents, and can be traced back to ages long anterior to Christianity, when we find them to involve ideas and practices common to many ancient religions, to the priest of the polytheist and to the Shaman of the nature-worshipper, are we not obliged to confess that the like are excrescences on Christianity, parasitic growths of which it had better be rid?[1]

would have been gratified by permission to indulge a taste for symbolism and a love of archaisms—and the more they had read the judgment, the less their real gain would have appeared; the other would have been able to quote the authority of the chief representative of the Church of England in insisting that the ceremonies in dispute were unimportant, and without doctrinal significance. So long as it is understood that this ritual means no more than the expression of a desire that all things should be done decently and in order, that it only gratifies sentiment, and does not inculcate doctrine other than that of the Church of England, then I wish not to interfere with the liberty of my neighbour, provided I am not compelled to take part in what only distracts my mind and hinders my prayers.

[1] These concluding remarks are not intended to apply to the Church of England as a body, though some of its members, if their assertions and practices are to be taken seriously, cannot be excepted from them. That all things should be done decently and in order is an Apostolic precept which commends itself to all men of religious instinct; but the elaborate and histrionic functions now held in so much favour by a section of the clergy seem to me much more likely

This is the conclusion to which, I think, many besides myself will be led before long, if they believe that the God of nature and of man is one and the same, and that methods generally identical are to be employed in the search for truth, whether in science or in theology, allowance being made for certain inherent differences; for in the latter, induction must be founded on indirect experiment or on general observation, while in the former the one may be direct and the other particular.

But by these scientific methods, as it seems to me, neither the leading historic facts nor the true spiritual element in Christianity will be altered. Science cannot forbid me to prostrate myself before that Almighty Personal Power which underlies all phenomena; it cannot reason me out of my consciousness of the need of a Spiritual Helper, and of the possi-

to foster superstition than to encourage devotion. For instance, in the *Directorium Anglicanum* (which, as it has reached a fourth edition, must be regarded with considerable favour among the clergy), we find included among the directions for the celebration of the Eucharist the " Cautels of the Mass," and stress is laid upon their value. Some of the directions in the said "cautels" seem to me much more like extracts from a book of magic than directions for due order in the worship of Him Who is revealed to us in the words of Christ and of His Apostles.

bility of some kind of communion with Him. No doubt it brings before my mind more distinctly the difficulties in accepting certain facts which are inseparable from the Christian creed; but, notwithstanding these difficulties, when I contemplate the whole subject and remember the imperfection of our knowledge even of that order of which our senses can take cognizance, I can accept as literally true the history of the Incarnation and the Resurrection of the Lord Jesus, and can believe in the efficacy of prayer and in the action of forces in the spiritual order, which I can neither define nor comprehend.

We are, then, I think, witnessing the opening of another epoch of change, which will rid the Reformed Church of sundry narrow ideas and some superstitions, the heritage of older days, which, after a long slumber, have recently awakened to a strangely and lamentably vigorous life. But their hours are numbered. Touched by the Ithuriel spear of truth, viewed in the clear, if somewhat cold, light of science, their real nature will be revealed. Many a fair form will disclose the ugly visage of latent paganism, and the bright robe of symbolism will be changed into the rags of idolatry and the talismans of the Shaman. The generation to come will set more store upon the Master's words than upon the interpretation given to them some centuries afterwards, and will possess a creed which is both simpler and more truly Catholic; for it will think less of legal and ceremonial observances, and more of loving the Lord Jesus Christ, and of seeking, be it never so imperfectly, to tread the path which He has pointed out by His Life and His Death.

T. G. BONNEY.

Contents

THE PRESENT CONFLICT OF SCIENCE AND THEOLOGY (BOYLE LECTURES, No. I.).

Preached in the Chapel Royal, Whitehall.

"But where shall wisdom be found? and where is the place of understanding?"—JOB XXVIII. 12, ... 1

THE PRESENT CONFLICT OF SCIENCE AND THEOLOGY (BOYLE LECTURES, No. II.).

Preached in the Chapel Royal, Whitehall.

"I found an altar with this inscription, To the unknown God."—ACTS XVII. 23, ... 14

THE PRESENT CONFLICT OF SCIENCE AND THEOLOGY (BOYLE LECTURES, No. III.).

Preached in the Chapel Royal, Whitehall.

"God, Who at sundry times and in divers manners spake in times past unto the fathers by the prophets, hath in these last days spoken unto us by His Son."—HEB. I. 1, ... 29

THE PRESENT CONFLICT OF SCIENCE AND THEOLOGY (BOYLE LECTURES, No. IV.).

Preached in the Chapel Royal, Whitehall.

"I came forth from the Father, and am come into the world: again I leave the world, and go to the Father."—ST. JOHN XVI. 28, ... 44

THE PRESENT CONFLICT OF SCIENCE AND THEOLOGY (BOYLE LECTURES, No. V.).
Preached in the Chapel Royal, Whitehall.

PAGE

"*I delight in the Law of God after the inward man: but I see another law in my members, warring against the law of my mind, and bringing me into captivity to the law of sin which is in my members.*"—ROM. VII. 22, 23, . . 59

THE PRESENT CONFLICT OF SCIENCE AND THEOLOGY (BOYLE LECTURES, No. VI.).
Preached in the Chapel Royal, Whitehall.

"*The Lord passed by before him, and proclaimed, The Lord, The Lord God, merciful, and gracious, long-suffering, and abundant in goodness and truth, keeping mercy for thousands, forgiving iniquity and transgression and sin, and that will by no means clear the guilty; visiting the iniquity of the fathers upon the children, and upon the children's children.*"—EXOD. XXXIV. 6, 7, . 74

THE PRESENT CONFLICT OF SCIENCE AND THEOLOGY (BOYLE LECTURES, No. VII.).
Preached in the Chapel Royal, Whitehall.

"*Be not ignorant of this one thing, that one day is with the Lord as a thousand years, and a thousand years as one day. The Lord is not slack concerning His promise, as some men count slackness.*"—2 PET. III. 8, 9, . . 86

THE PRESENT CONFLICT OF SCIENCE AND THEOLOGY (BOYLE LECTURES, No. VIII.).
Preached in the Chapel Royal, Whitehall.

"*Remember how short my time is: wherefore hast Thou made all men in vain?*"—Ps. LXXXIX. 47, ... 98

THE THREEFOLD NATURE OF MAN.
Preached before the University of Cambridge.

"*May your spirit and soul and body be preserved entire, without blame, at the coming of our Lord Jesus Christ.*"—1 THESS. V. 23 (R.V.), . . . 114

THE INSPIRATION OF SCRIPTURE (No. I.).

Preached at St. Peter's, Vere Street.

PAGE

"*All Scripture is given by inspiration of God, and is profitable for doctrine, for reproof, for correction, for instruction in righteousness.*"—2 TIM. III. 16, . 135

THE INSPIRATION OF SCRIPTURE (No. II.).

Preached at St. Peter's, Vere Street.

" *Your fathers dwelt on the other side of the flood in old time, even Terah, the father of Abraham, and the father of Nachor : and they served other gods.*"
—JOSH. XXIV. 2, ... 148

THE GROWTH OF JESUS (No. I.).

Preached at St. Peter's, Vere Street.

"*And Jesus increased in wisdom and stature, and in favour with God and man.*"—ST. LUKE II. 52, ... 162

THE GROWTH OF JESUS (No. II.).

Preached at St. Peter's, Vere Street.

"*And Jesus increased in wisdom and stature, and in favour with God and man.*"—ST. LUKE II. 52, ... 175

THE GOSPEL OF ST. PAUL.

Preached in Westminster Abbey.

"*If in this life only we have hoped in Christ, we are of all men most pitiable.*"—1 COR. XV. 19 (R.V.), ... 187

THE DEMONIACS OF GADARA.

Preached at St. Peter's, Vere Street.

"*So the devils besought Him, saying, If Thou cast us out, suffer us to go away into the herd of swine.*"—ST. MATT. VIII. 31, ... 203

THE MIRACLES OF APOSTOLIC AND MEDIÆVAL TIMES.

Preached for the Christian Evidence Society.

"There shall arise false Christs and false prophets, and shall show great signs and wonders, insomuch that, if it were possible, they shall deceive the very elect."—St. Matt. xxiv. 24, ... 218

THE RAISING OF THE WIDOW'S SON.

Preached at St. Peter's, Vere Street.

"Jesus said, Young man, I say unto thee, Arise. And he that was dead sat up, and began to speak."—St. Luke vii. 14, 15, ... 231

PATIENCE IN WORK.

Preached at the Ordination in Manchester Cathedral.

"Be patient therefore, brethren, unto the coming of the Lord. Behold, the husbandman waiteth for the precious fruit of the earth, and hath long patience for it, until he receive the early and latter rain."—St. James v. 7, . . . 243

THE LILIES OF THE FIELD.

Preached in Shoreditch Church.

"Consider the lilies of the field, how they grow; they toil not, neither do they spin: and yet I say unto you, That even Solomon in all his glory was not arrayed like one of these."—St. Matt. vi. 28, 29, ... 256

THE ORIGIN OF EVIL 269

Lecture at St. Philip's, Regent Street, founded on a paper read at Sion College.

THE PRESENT CONFLICT OF SCIENCE AND THEOLOGY (BOYLE LECTURES, NO. I.).[1]

"But where shall wisdom be found? and where is the place of understanding?"—JOB XXVIII. 12.

WE are living in anxious times, and who will venture to predict what event the next quarter of a century will bring forth? Is our nation, is the civilized part of the world, approaching an epoch of convulsion, the birth-throes of a new order, like that which, about a century since, shattered the ancient *régime* and changed the face of Europe; or will the clouds of discord, war, and revolution roll away harmlessly as the light broadens and brightens to the more perfect day? Will the faith of Christendom be once more exposed to proscription and persecution, or only saved from this by contemptuous and almost universal abandonment; or may we reply in the words of the suffering patriarch, and with a trust strengthened by continuous revelation, "God hath said to man,

[1] Preached in the Chapel Royal, Whitehall, on the Sunday after Ascension Day, 1890.

Behold the fear of the Lord, that is wisdom; and to depart from evil is understanding"?

I purpose to speak in these lectures of one of the above-named possibilities, though they are all the outcome of the same causes, and the questions, I believe, will receive an answer in like accents, whether it be for cursing or for blessing.

The outlook in reference to the future of our religious belief seems to me very fairly expressed in some words which caught my eye a few hours before I was called upon to undertake the responsible duty of addressing this congregation. "There are," said the author,[1] "two movements in our time which are frequently confounded, the 'No Theology' and the 'New Theology,' both having the same origin, springing from the same intellectual unrest and discontent with the past. These," he says, and rightly, I think, in the main, "are the remedies proposed for the present condition of confusion and disorganization, which may be summarized in a popular expression—the conflict of religion and science." Real or baseless, this conflict indubitably exists; it cannot, then, be wasted time to endeavour to ascertain its causes, to investigate their validity, and to consider the remedies which have been proposed.

[1] Lyman Abbott, *The Forum*, April, 1890.

This conflict—and its province is not limited to theology—is the outcome of two principles, as we may call them, which at first sight appear to be completely antagonistic—reason and authority. In an ideal condition there would be no real opposition between these; in the actual this is often inevitable, but it is vastly accentuated by the mistakes of mankind. It would hardly be too much to say that the conflict is as old as civilization, and, in beings such as we are, is an almost necessary concomitant of growth.

In the field of religion—than which, as the motive-force in our conduct, there is nothing more important—this conflict, though veiled more decorously than heretofore, is still active. We may symbolize the tendencies which actuate the two parties as the scientific and the ecclesiastical. They are now, perhaps, more distinctly antagonistic than was the case a generation since, because the vast progress which, during this interval, has been made by science, using the word in a wide sense, has led to a fresh demand for enlarging the province of reason, and this has been met in some quarters by a revival of ecclesiastical pretensions and a recrudescence of superstition.

Of this conflict different solutions have been

proposed. By one party of extremists it is predicted that reason will dispel the illusions of faith, which will be banished into outer darkness by the light of the no-theology. The opposite party proclaim the coming good time when unsanctified reason will be dragged in chains behind the car of triumphant faith. Some are for a compromise, and for a more accurate delimitation of the provinces of science and of theology; while others maintain that no such definite distinction is possible, and that the theology of the future must be based on an admission of their unity of origin, even though a diversity of function may be recognized.

The notion of antagonistic principles of good and evil is a very old one. It has its attractions for some minds, for it offers an explanation of phenomena which at first sight is so simple. But its philosophic difficulties are numerous; its theological are of the gravest kind. On the present occasion, however, I need not linger to discuss Manichæan ideas as to the antagonism of matter and God. Nevertheless, we shall do well to remember that much popular Christianity and popular belief is unconsciously tainted with Manichæan dualism. Language is not seldom heard in relation to nature which, if strictly interpreted, would mean that the world was virtually, if not actually, the work of an Evil One. This, however, I may discuss on a future occasion, and so I pass on to the question of the separability of science and religion.

But it may be reasonably asked what is meant by the term religion, for it is used in more than one sense. To some, religion means "cultus," or the practice of observances; to others, "creed," or a collection of formulated opinions as to the Unseen Being, or what is generally meant by theology; to others, "reverence or love for the ethical ideal, and the desire to realize that ideal in life."[1] To myself the word expresses all these, the last-named being the leading conception, though I cannot wholly separate it from the second—that of knowledge—real or supposed, because my ethical ideal is not a mere summary of detached qualities, gathered from observation, but a person, or, at any rate, a power which I can only contemplate as personified, whatever its true nature may be. I would employ the term "theology," had not this, in my opinion, become too much specialized, and separated, in practice, though not in theory, from ethics. Many persons would tell us that the methods of science and religion are different, the one being the province of reason, the other of faith; that their ends are different, that of the one being the

[1] Professor Huxley, *Nineteenth Century*, February, 1889.

acquirement of knowledge, that of the other the exercise of the emotions.

At first sight the distinction seems valid. The conclusions of science, it will be said, are capable of verification; its foundation is experiment. When it ceases to be the inductive treatment of facts, it is no longer science. Faith is trust in an unseen, and in some sense unknown, Power, Whom by ourselves we could not discover, Who must in some way have made Himself known to us. Thus its basis is revelation. But how is a revelation made? It must be either direct, by a personal intuition or some kind of vision, or indirect, in the form of a message transmitted through a fellow-man. In either case how am I to know that I am not the victim of some deception? for the possibility of this is a matter of experience. If I am directed to compare the supposed revelation with beliefs already accepted, this only shifts the difficulty a stage further back, because I must ascertain why these were accepted.

Inquiry on that point would receive some such answer as this: "They were accepted at first because the teacher appeared to be endowed with exceptional authority of some kind, and because it was felt that his doctrines supplied a want which had been hitherto unsatisfied. Since then experience has shown this satisfaction to have been real, not illusory, and the new creed has proved to be a motive-force of high value." But all this demands the exercise of reason; it is a process strictly scientific, for it is a series of inductions founded on ascertained facts. If, then, faith is to be anything more than a mere play of emotion, to which the disciple of the no-theology would restrict it, there cannot be any province from which reason can be absolutely excluded.

But I may be asked, Do you consider that faith may be subjected to experiment, like the conclusions of science; that, for instance, we can verify the accuracy of our belief by the results of prayer, a test which has been propounded in all seriousness, and is regarded by some votaries of science as a fair challenge? Certainly not. Such a challenge, such an idea, results from a common but restricted view of science. There are undoubtedly branches of science where each induction can be tested, as often as desired, by direct experiment. A denial can be met by a demonstration. Such, for instance, is the case in chemistry. Did any one deny that water was produced by the combination of two particular gases, his error could be demonstrated by analysis and synthesis till he was silenced. But even in such a science there are stages where direct demonstration becomes less and less possible, while in some sciences it has but a small place. In geology, for instance, the demonstration must be to a large extent indirect. The processes of nature are inferred from observing them in different stages on separate occasions, not from the continuous watching of any one from its beginning to its end. We venture to pronounce upon the past history of the earth, though no man was there to mark its changes or record the results. We people it with living creatures, not because the exact likeness of them can now be discovered, but from the analogies of the fossil remnants to the parts of existing organisms. In this science, the leading principles are already firmly established, and yet they are inductions mainly founded on indirect observations, not on direct experiments.

But we may be told that science does not admit of authority. It does this, in my opinion, far more than is generally supposed. We accept much on the testimony of others, because no man can begin everything *de novo* for himself. Life is far too short for this. Still it may be said that, if doubt arise, every step of the inquiry may be rigorously tested. To a large extent this is true, but it will still be found that many generalizations can hardly be subjected to this process. A personal element enters into an induction more than is commonly supposed. It results from a mental process which often cannot be formulated, from the accumulated experience and cultivated intellect of the individual. The lightning-flash of scientific genius, as it may be termed—that which makes all the difference between great men and small men in science—has much authority with a student, who defers to it, unless he feels that he possesses facts and an experience which were not at the command of his predecessor.

This, then, brings us to the special difficulty of the present epoch. It has not arisen from new demands on the part of theologians. Doubtless they are largely to blame for the origin of the conflict; their efforts to subjugate the reason and tyrannize over the intellect have often deserved the severest censure; they have sometimes gone near to making Christianity a curse instead of a blessing. By this time, however, most of them have gained wisdom from experience, though the voices of a foolish few can still be heard in noisy objurgation; but the particular phase of the difficulty at the present time is the outcome, I believe, of a particular phase in the history of science itself.

During the last thirty or forty years marvellous progress has been made in the mechanical arts. As one result, the instruments and appliances for experimental research have been greatly improved and augmented. Direct demonstration, direct investigation, have become possible in many matters where formerly only indirect proofs could be obtained. Tests of extreme delicacy, instruments of extreme precision, can be employed, of which our predecessors hardly ventured to dream. As a natural consequence, there is sometimes a disposition to enlarge unduly the province of direct experiment, and to over-estimate the importance of its results. Thus arises a tendency either to believe nothing which cannot be tested by this method, or to suppose that a statement of the sequences of a process is tantamount to a discovery of its cause. To go back to my former illustration. It may be demonstrated to me that oxygen and hydrogen, under certain circumstances, combine to form water, but I am aware that under other circumstances they might produce something possessing very different properties, and the fact alone brings me no nearer to ascertaining why this or that environment is needful for the result.

There is also another cause, the outcome of a tendency from which science itself is beginning to suffer. The perfection of our instruments and the wealth of nature, which makes almost the humblest organism a microcosm, have induced many students to undertake minutely elaborated investigations in a narrow field of research. A single animal or a single limited group of animals, or some similarly restricted question, becomes the labour of a life. Over-concentration of attention on detail leads to the loss of all sense of proportion. The comparative faculty suffers, a breadth of view becomes impossible, so that in modern science we not unfrequently meet with investigators, the value of whose inductive work bears an inverse ratio to its conscientious minuteness. We are beginning to be told, even in scientific circles, that we have plenty of microscopists, but few naturalists, many specialists, but few capable of generalization; that such a man as Darwin could hardly be produced in the rising generation, for he would be exhausted by the infinity of detail, or smothered under the mass of literature. But a few years since, one, whose authority cannot be disputed,[1] publicly declared that science was now in danger of the fate of Tarpeia, that of perishing beneath the weight of the gifts heaped upon her; gifts, he might have gone on to say, among which, as in her case, the metal of little worth far outweighed the gold.

Even the use of the term "science" indicates a similar influence. By many it is tacitly restricted to such

[1] Professor Huxley, Presidential Address to the Royal Society (*Proceedings of the Royal Society*, vol. xxxix. p. 295).

subjects as can be treated experimentally, in forgetfulness that all inductive treatment of facts is science. Thus there is not only a science of chemistry or of physics, of biology or of geology, but also a science of language and of history; nay, there is even a science of theology, so that the hard and fast line which is so often drawn cannot be maintained.

Hence it has become possible for the theologian to carry the war into the opposite camp; to demonstrate that, by employing the method of argument which is used against him, it would be possible to discredit most facts of history, throw doubts upon many conclusions of science, and plunge ourselves at last in one vast agnostic slough of despond, in which we should be sure of nothing, except perhaps our own state of discomfort, and even here might be uncertain how far this were not an illusion.

It is, then, my intention in these lectures to follow up the lines of thought which I have now briefly indicated—to insist that the conflict of theology and science is only man's putting asunder of what God hath joined; that the difficulties which are often felt at the present day cannot be solved by the method of the no-theology any more than they can be satisfied, unless we repudiate the use of reason, by blind submission to authority; that we are not compelled by any logical necessity to follow either the path which leads to a general negation of religious belief, or that which leads to unreasoning credulity; that here, as so often in human affairs, the *via media* is the safe, because it is the right way. I will not call it the way of compromise, because I do not hold that the due apportionment of their rights to either party in a dispute can properly receive that name. While I admit that science and religion are now often in conflict, I hold that the time will come when they will be in alliance, because each is a manifestation of the same Power; each is an aspect, though different, of the same Person; each reveals to man the same God, Who would otherwise be unknown.

THE PRESENT CONFLICT OF SCIENCE AND THEOLOGY (BOYLE LECTURES, NO. II.).[1]

"I found an altar with this inscription, To the unknown God."—ACTS XVII. 23.

MORE than eighteen centuries since, in the focus of culture and intellect, this stone bore to the passer-by its silent testimony. The precise significance of the inscription we do not know, but read in the light, if so we may use the word, of the present age, its words strike a note of unconscious prophecy, utter a sigh of mournful pathos. More than eighteen centuries have passed, and amid all the triumphs of civilization, all the increase of wisdom, we are told, in tones yet more emphatic than those of philosophers of Greece, that God is, and must ever be, unknown. We are only so far wiser than the men of Athens as to deem it an act of superstitious folly to raise an altar to His honour.

There is, indeed, a sense in which the words must ever be true; the finite cannot measure the infinite,

[1] Preached in the Chapel Royal, Whitehall, on Whitsunday, 1890.

the less cannot comprehend the incommensurably greater. Man's knowledge of God must be partial, imperfect, relative; but the main question is, Can he attain even to this stage, or is the pursuit only that of an *ignis fatuus;* is the hope which has sustained myriads of the noblest spirits in this dark world only a fond delusion? Nature and man, science and history, present to us a host of problems which crave an answer from every thoughtful mind. "Whence comest thou? whither goest thou?" may be asked of everything, of every personality which confronts us. We stand, as it were, in the presence of some vast machine, marvellous in its complication, wondrous in the beauty of its products. Yet is this all? Is there no meaning in this kaleidoscopic alternation of birth and death, no bourne to which they tend, no Heart to which we may be the hands; but only an omnipotent energy, without conscious purpose, without all-perfect love?

Among the solutions which have been proposed for this problem, two are attractive from their apparent simplicity: the one is named Atheism, the other Pantheism. The former "repudiates the theological doctrine of a Creator and a Moral Providence. It admits no other existence than matter and force, and of these it offers no explanation. They are, and that suffices."[1] But this solution need not now be discussed, for I believe that the majority of thoughtful men will acquiesce in Comte's opinion that "atheism is the most irrational form of metaphysics, because it propounds as the solution of an insoluble enigma the hypothesis least capable of proof, least simple, and least plausible."[2] Even if they cannot accept the solution which has satisfied the Christian, they will admit that, to quote the words of a well-known leader of their school, "One truth must grow ever clearer—the truth that there is an Inscrutable Existence everywhere manifested, to which he [man] can neither find nor conceive either beginning or end. Amid the mysteries, which become the more mysterious the more they are thought about, there will remain the one absolute certainty, that he is ever in presence of an Infinite and Eternal Energy, from which all things proceed."[3]

Pantheism asserts that all is God. This is an hypothesis which at first sight seems far more attractive, but its difficulties increase the more it is scrutinized. That all is *of God* we readily admit, but to assert that "God is everything, and everything is

---

[1] F. Harrison, in *Fortnightly Review*, vol. xiv. p. 145.
[2] *Idem*, p. 146.
[3] Herbert Spencer, *Ecclesiastical Institutions*, § 660.

God," ultimately breaks down all differences between right and wrong, and "ends," as it has been justly said, "in identifying the worshipper with the Deity." The marks of imperfection, the signs of contest of the lower with the higher, are writ too large in nature for us to accept this hypothesis as a permanent solution of the difficulty, though we admit that it is rather an overstatement, or a very partial aspect, of a truth than a proposition inherently false. Nevertheless, it is the outcome of a confusion of thought, which might find a parallel in science in the failure to distinguish between force and energy, and while it claims to be the esoteric doctrine of polytheism, it leads practically, as experience has shown, to the least mystical forms of this creed.

But by many who are honestly perplexed at the difficulties of the problem a refuge has been sought, especially at the present day, in what is called Agnosticism. He who adopts this position may be defined as one "who, having honestly sought to know, acquiesces in ignorance, and avows it as the best practical solution of a profound but inscrutable problem." He "protests against any dogma respecting creation at all, and takes his stand deliberately on ignorance."[1]

It is a position curiously different from that assumed

[1] F. Harrison, *Fortnightly Review*, vol. xlv. p. 144.

by a worker in science, and it is expressive of a spirit directly opposite to that by which he is animated. Write over the doors of our laboratories, "Leave hope behind, ye who enter here;" write large upon their walls, "No man can raise the veil of Nature," and there would be a speedy end to progress, a paralysis of mind for the most earnest of students. It is hope which is the mainspring of his work; this nerves him to shun delights and live laborious days, to watch and to wait patiently in the presence of the most tangled web of perplexities and apparent contradictions, confident that some day, by another who has built on his foundation if not by himself, the hidden clue, the long-sought truth, will be discovered. "I give it up; it is an inscrutable enigma." Where would science now be, if its followers had acted on this maxim?

But, it will be said, the analogy is misleading, because, in investigations concerning subjects which theology professes to treat, we are debarred by the nature of the case from making use of the methods of science. This objection, however, appears to me due to a misunderstanding. From such investigations—as from all where direct experiment is not applicable—the instruments of research are excluded, but not the inductive treatment of facts, not the science, which is wider than the walls of the laboratory.

Agnosticism owes its strength at the present day to the following causes: First—as I have previously said [1] —to that misuse of theology which, for want of a better name, may be called ecclesiasticism. It is the result of a protest, in itself right and honest, against such a dictum as this: "Let us maintain before we have proved;"[2] or this, "Religious error is, in itself, of an immoral nature." There is, indeed, a sense in which the one statement may be justified, the other reduced to a truism, but this is not the one usually intended or understood. That ecclesiasticism is the real foe is admitted by a living advocate of agnosticism, who speaks as follows: "With scientific theology agnosticism has no quarrel. . . . But, as between agnosticism and ecclesiasticism, or, as our neighbours across the Channel call it, clericalism, there can be neither peace nor truce."[3] Be it so. I have read and even seen too much of the mischief wrought by presumptuous ignorance and sacerdotal arrogance to desire to hold back the axe from that parasitic growth, for after its destruction the tree of theology and true religion would bear fruit more abundantly than heretofore.

[1] Sermon I., p. 3.
[2] The late Cardinal Newman, quoted by Professor Huxley, *Nineteenth Century*, vol. xxv. p. 939.
[3] Professor Huxley, *ut supra*.

Another cause, for which the same spirit is largely responsible, is an erroneous view of the nature and province of revelation. It is assumed—not on one side only—that when knowledge is communicated to man concerning something which he is incapable of discovering for himself, the fact that this proceeds from the source of Truth compels us to suppose that the human element must be eliminated from the messenger, that he must become an infallible authority on every department of human knowledge, and that there must be nothing in the message which is relative to the hearers or appropriate to a progressive system of teaching. Thus, it is assumed, a revelation to men of a different race and a lower civilization than our own must be in terms which would satisfy the present generation. This demand I pass by for the present, contenting myself with remarking that it involves an assumption which appears to me unwarranted, inasmuch as it makes the present century the standard for all ages, and tacitly assumes, in so doing, that man has now attained to his full development, intellectual and spiritual.

Difficulties as to the evidence for Christianity are, at the present day, another cause of agnosticism. Of these, one class relates to the authenticity or genuineness of its records; the other, to the fundamental idea of Christianity, viz. its so-called miraculous origin. The former has received so much attention of late that on the present occasion I feel justified in refraining from discussing it in detail, and in contenting myself with remarking that the result of scholarly research during the last quarter of a century has been to strengthen rather than to weaken the historic value of the early records of Christianity, and to indicate that, if it be an illusion or a fraud, it was this from the very first.

I pass on, then, to the latter—the difficulties as to the so-called miraculous origin of Christianity. These I fully appreciate. I admit that they cannot be met by direct methods, by experiment or demonstration; but I believe that they are greatly lessened by indirect treatment, by arguments, negative rather than positive.

For the present I shall restrict myself to one point in the discussion: the *à priori* probability or improbability of a revelation to man. If I assume the universe to be the work of God, I trust that I may also assume that He has not ceded, either of good will or by force of conquest, this particular planet to any hostile power. If so, the book of nature which lies open before us is either a collection of blank pages or a mode of revelation. An alternative, in favour, I believe, with some, that it is a palimpsest writ large by the hand of Satan, seems to me beset with such serious difficulties, so derogatory to the honour of God, as hardly to need serious consideration. If the pages are blank, then the study of nature is wasted time. To this, however, those who have tried to read that wondrous volume will hesitate to subscribe. Assuming, then, that there be not only an Infinite Energy, but also mind, purpose, love, personality of a kind—the ideas, in short, which to most of us are embodied in the word "God"—we have in nature the expression of Himself in a form capable of being perceived by us. Suppose, for a moment, this were the only means by which we could acquire knowledge of Him. Spirit is not directly cognizable by man. This word implies a mode of existence which cannot be tested by senses fitted to deal only with the material. Hence it is not a subject for direct experiment, but for indirect induction. To use the well-known simile, it is inferred from its operations, as the wind, which we cannot see, can be recognized by its effects. This being so, nature is a mode of revelation, and thus may be made a basis of induction. What, then, do we learn from nature? First, it discloses a mighty and far-reaching system of education. The present is the offspring of the past—the heir of its opportunities, of its progress, even of its errors. Step by step we see unrolled the ancestral pedigree of the varied forms of life which people this earth, as science bids bone join to bone, and the breath return to the dust, which has been gathered again from the four winds of heaven. We see the same law of growth and of development which has been concentrated in the brief span of our earlier life, operating through myriads of years, as race after race of higher powers and more perfect organization comes forth, fulfils its time, then passes away or falls into the background, to give place to something yet nearer to perfection. Can we say that the limit has been reached; that further progress, physical or intellectual, is impossible? This might, with equal reason, have been asserted at any one stage in the process of evolution; it would have been repudiated by the teaching of experience and the logic of facts. What more reason have we in denying now the possibility of anything further, as we do if we assert that man's doom is to seek, but never to find?

But in reading the book of nature, we are conscious before long of an incompleteness. Its teaching is one-sided; it favours the development of the animal propensities rather than of the ethical faculties. This was only to be expected, for life is conditioned by environment. In this world, before we can think, or learn, or purpose, we must be kept alive and in a condition to use the faculties which we possess, whatever may be their cause or their tendency. The child learns first and of necessity the laws of life, because total ignorance of these would mean death; and then those of thought, without the knowledge of which he cannot be perfectly a man. The race receives from the natural world instruction in physical laws, given with an emphasis more marked than in any other branch of learning.

But, then, history indicates no less clearly a moral development in the race. That is a fact which demands an explanation, and this is difficult if we insist on no other teaching than that of the physical universe. Moral development and physical development are not always compatible. They are the outcome, as it seems to me, of tendencies which often are distinctly antagonistic. The law of the former is, sacrifice self for others; the law of the latter is, sacrifice others for self. Yet moral progress is a fact in the world's history, though certainly the principles to which it is due are not inculcated by the physical order, and can only, at most, be indirectly inferred from it. Hence, it seems an improbable hypothesis to ascribe moral progess to that origin only, and it is simpler to regard this as the operation of a Power which makes for righteousness.

But if we admit the idea of making for righteousness we imply an Influence, and indirectly the work of a Teacher, to whom mankind stands in a relation different from that of other beings in the physical world.

We find, also, that in man desires and capacities exist—whatever may be their origin—which can only be satisfied by a sense of relationship with a Power far higher than himself; a faculty of religiousness, as we might call it; the need of an object of worship, of an ideal Being which is to be like the sun of man's moral system. Which is the more reasonable, to regard this as the outcome of his comparatively rudimentary stage of intellectual development—a mere transient emotion, like that of a child for a toy—or an impulse to seek One Who may be found ? Nature and history, as it seems to me, teach us that demand does not generally exist where there is no possibility of supply. Such existence would be contrary to that economy which in this world's order seems to regulate the expenditure of energy. If there are physical wants and moral wants which may be satisfied, physical ideals and moral ideals which may be attained, upon what *à priori* grounds can it be asserted that the religious wants and the religious ideals are all illusions ?

I venture, then, to put this question to the agnostic. You admit that the world is a place of education for me considered not only as an animal, but also as a being endowed with reason. I believe, indeed, you would go so far as to admit the probability of its being also a place of moral education. What, I ask, is to be the motive-force in the last? I might put it thus: "Am I brought up or scrambled up?" And, if brought up, is this for a purpose—I speak as a man—or without a purpose? If you affirm the latter, your position is at least intelligible; but we must not shrink from its consequences. Then the tale of our lives is quickly told: the hope of a personal immortality is an illusion; beyond the grave is nothingness. I may regret it, but if I am to be limited to the direct teaching of nature, no other conclusion seems to me possible. Her reply sounds to me clear and distinct: "Death is the end of life." If I limit myself to the results of my work in the laboratory or in the field, I find no "hope of pardon or redress behind the veil." I must admit that my life is "as futile as frail." But as a rule you will not go so far as this. Concerning personal immortality, concerning the soul, as we call it, you will make no statement, negative or positive; you will only say that you know nothing about it. To deny the possibility of its existence would be as unphilosophical as to affirm. Indeed, you would admit, I believe, that our hypothesis solves many of the enigmas presented by the order of this world, and supplements what appear to be defects.

If that be so, then I contend that my position is the more reasonable, the more in accord with the inductive habit of science. I see in man capacities physical, moral, and religious; I see provision made, as I may term it, for the education of two of these; I see also that wants do not normally exist where their gratification is impossible. The longing after God exists; is it man's doom in this one respect to stretch in vain lame hands of faith, and grope "upon the great world's altar stairs that slope through darkness," not up to God, but up to the vacancy of unsatisfied desire?

Can you offer us no better ideal of God than the choice of this alternative? Either He is merely an Infinite Energy, the underlying source of every phenomenon, in some sense, of every aspiration of our being, before which, however, we are nothing more than the most tiny ephemeral insects are to the sunbeam—it causes them to dance, but recks not whether they do it or no—or He is One Who reposes in eternal calm, far away from the world which He has made, smiling perhaps now and then at our blindfold stumbles in a fruitless search. Truly a hard Master; truly a Being very remote from every ideal of altruistic excellence and moral perfection,—ideals to which you are as earnest as we in urging on mankind; truly a centre of repellent rather than of attractive Force. Might we not fairly retort, when you frankly confess that you can offer, in satisfaction of our wants, nothing better than this pitiless Power to guide us through life's trials and difficulties—

> "Let us alone. What pleasure can we have
> To war with evil? Is there any peace
> In ever climbing up the climbing wave?
> All things have rest, and ripen toward the grave
> In silence; ripen, fall, and cease:
> Give us long rest or death, dark death, or dreamful ease."[1]

[1] Tennyson, *The Lotos Eaters*.

THE PRESENT CONFLICT OF SCIENCE AND THEOLOGY (BOYLE LECTURES, No. III.).[1]

"God, Who at sundry times and in divers manners spake in times past unto the fathers by the prophets, hath in these last days spoken unto us by His Son."—HEB. I. 1.

REVELATION, or no revelation; the guidance towards a far-off light, or the blind groping in a hopeless darkness, the whisper of a voice, or the eternal silence;—which is the portion of our race? This is the question which it behoves us to answer; and a negative reply would make it needless to discuss the evidence for or against Christianity. Agnosticism admits, as we have seen, that the end of scientific thought and research is the conviction that we are "ever in the presence of an Infinite and Eternal Energy, from which all things proceed." It appears also to admit that, as an effect of the environment, or by the discipline of life, higher faculties, clearer conceptions, and more profound insights are developed in the human race, which render it more and

[1] Preached at the Chapel Royal, Whitehall, on Trinity Sunday, 1890.

more capable of formulating for itself an explanation, if such there be, of the Ultimate Reality. To all this, as Christians, we can heartily assent. We admit that in all the operations of God, as we prefer to call the Infinite Energy, the same principle and similar methods are exhibited; that in religious ideas and conceptions there is a process of growth which may be termed natural, of evolution which appears to be conditioned by the environment; that, in the spiritual as in the natural order, the law of continuity prevails in those phenomena with which our minds are capable of dealing. But the main difference between us is this: that to the agnostic, revelation, if he permit me to use the term, indicates a process wholly continuous, the result of means which are neither more nor less beyond comprehension than any other in operation on this earth; while to myself the process, at least in its initiation, exhibits discontinuity. In it the Divine Energy acts, as it were, on a plane different from that to which we are accustomed. Thus it produces different results—just as in nature the introduction of a force hitherto inoperative would modify phenomena; and it has for its effect the acquirement of knowledge which, without this special influence, would have been unattainable. If I rightly understand, the agnostic regards the rise and progress of the religious idea or ideal, like the advance of philosophy or science, as beneficial to the race in proportion to its truth, which, however, can never be more than relative. Its results also, whether for good or evil, must be limited to this life; for of anything further we neither have, nor can have, any knowledge. But the Christian hopes, nay, believes, that when the Unknown Energy is manifested as a novel Force—which he calls "Spiritual Power"— and co-operates with the processes which are termed "natural," it produces in men a result which he can only describe as a new birth, even to a life which is eternal.

This belief, this expectation, is commonly judged unscientific. Obviously it cannot be tested by direct experiment, but we are not thereby justified in rejecting it, until we see whether or not it is discordant with the inductions which may be drawn from facts which are part of human experience.

The author from whom I have more than once quoted affirms that "civilized men have no innate tendency to form religious ideas."[1] The proposition appears to me one which can be neither proved nor disproved satisfactorily, but for our present purpose I am content that it be assumed. Well, then, civilized man has formed religious ideas, and these sometimes

[1] Herbert Spencer, *Ecclesiastical Institutions*, § 672.

exhibit very remarkable complexity. How came he by them? They are, it will be said, an evolution from a group of fancies which have an origin perfectly natural. But if so, it appears to me an anomaly that every marked advance towards the religious ideal should exhibit in its initial stage a kind of discontinuity. Even when, by investigation, we succeed in discovering some of its components, these appear, like certain chemical constituents, to have been lying for long, side by side, without action or result, until by some unknown stimulus, like the passage of an electric spark, they are brought into combination and initiate a series of consequences.

The history also of the new ideal is hardly such as we should expect, if it were the result of processes merely natural. It is one of desperate struggle for existence; and its foes may well be called those of its own household. It meets with the most bitter opposition in the very quarters which would have seemed its natural home. It conquers, as it appears, against all odds, by its truth, assuming that there be such a thing, and that you can test it like any other working hypothesis. Granted that there is here a survival of the fittest, yet this is not in accordance with the ordinary law of evolution, where the victory results from the special adaptation of the organism to the environments. Here, if one may so express it, the organism conquers the environment and becomes the master of circumstance.

It must always be borne in mind that, in referring any result to natural causes, we do not the less regard it as the outcome of the Divine Power. If it be a result of the Infinite and Eternal Energy, as it is admitted to be by the philosopher, it is in the language of the Christian the work of God. In using the word "natural," we mean no more than that the event, instead of being, as heretofore, an isolated phenomenon, a consequent without an antecedent, now falls into its place in a sequence of phenomena. But even then the discovery does not take us far. We have been able to make an additional step in correlation and classification; we are no nearer to a real discovery of cause.

Some, however, may say that the Christian cannot shelter himself under a general statement of this kind—that, by adopting the name and accepting the consequences which it entails, namely, a belief in certain alleged historical events, he commits himself to the truth of a story which contains a miraculous element, and so puts himself outside the pale of science. There is a certain amount of truth in the objection. I am prepared to admit that if Christ were nothing more than an ordinary man, if it were only true that He died upon the cross, if He did not rise from the dead, then there would be no essential difference between our creed and other ethical systems. In the life of Christ, I admit, there were incidents which find no parallel in the history of ordinary men, phenomena contrary to common experience, inexplicable by known causes—incidents, in short, which we term miraculous.

This position appears to many to be wholly unscientific. Let us endeavour to ascertain, so far as time permits, how far their opinion can be justified. Laws and miracle are commonly assumed to be contradictory terms. This assumption is often made by both parties in the controversy. But the difficulty thereby created is gratuitous; it arises from an anthropomorphic conception of the Divine Being and the inevitable imperfections of human language. In referring to Him, we permit, unwisely often, the use of such terms as "interference," "change of purpose," and the like, we allow ourselves to think of Him—how inadequately!—as of a kind of head engineer of this world's machinery, changing and altering, mending and improving, moving this and stopping that, so as to hinder one result and bring about another. God is not a man, and every anthropomorphic conception, inevitable though it may be as a symbol of thought, is a misleading conception. Law, of which we sometimes talk as though it were antagonistic to God—law, I say, is but man's induction from watching the sequence of the phenomena of the Divine Power, the modes of manifestation of the Unknown and Infinite Energy. The laws of nature were not fixed by some necessity, and imposed upon the demiurge of the universe to be now and then eluded, or even, under specially favourable circumstances, overruled by him; they are nothing more than our statement of a chain of sequences. Cause and effect must always stand in a fixed relation—to say this is a mere truism—but it is an unwarrantable assumption to assert that our view of any sequence is always the correct one. Regarded in its relation to the physical order, miracle is only a relative term. In one sense nothing is miraculous, for everything is an outcome of the same Energy, of which law is the expression, not the restraint; in another sense everything is miraculous, because we can never arrive at the Principle of Causation.

Physical miracles are not rare—phenomena which no doubt have a cause, but it is one which we have hitherto failed to discover. For instance, if there be one thing which on *à priori* grounds we might have reasonably expected, it is that any chemical element should be constant in its physical characters. Yet carbon, which is one of the commonest constituents in the substances known to us, assumes at least three distinct forms, each characterized by markedly different physical properties. It is now opaque and soft, now pellucid and the hardest of minerals; sometimes it exhibits the opacity and almost retains the softness of the one, while it assumes the distinct and separate crystal form of the other.

Take another case, where the result is produced by a cause apparently inadequate. Drop into a crucible of molten gold a pellet of lead, only one-thousandth part by weight, and the metal when cooled loses its usual properties and becomes brittle. Into a crucible of melting iron drop the same proportion of aluminium, and "the pasty mass will become as fluid as water."[1] These results are miraculous to me, for I can find no real explanation of them.[2] For this I

---

[1] W. Anderson, Presidential address to Section G., British Association, 1889. See also the important researches of Professor Roberts-Austen and others referred to by Sir F. Abel in his Presidential address to the same body at Leeds, 1890.

[2] I am, of course, aware that the researches of Professor Roberts-Austen and others tend to establish a connection between these results and the atomic volumes of the elements, in accordance with Mendeljeff's law, but I cannot say that, to my mind, important and interesting as this induction is, it amounts to an *explanation*.

must assume properties in the constituent molecules or ultimate atoms which I cannot comprehend. But it will be said these are not miraculous, because they can be repeated as often as we please. Quite true: they are not so in our rough and ready classification; they cease to be miracles when we know how to do them—that is to say, the test of the miraculous is in the intellectual standpoint of the particular age. Its sphere contracts, or perhaps I should say recedes, with the advance of education.

This argument, however, need not be carried further, for some of our critics frankly admit that "physical science has had nothing directly to do with the criticism of the gospels; it is wholly incompetent to furnish demonstrative evidence that any statement made in these histories is untrue. Indeed, modern physiology can find parallels in nature for events of apparently the most supernatural kind recounted in some of those histories."[1]

Our difficulties, then, by this last concession, are narrowed down to these: (1) the validity of the historic evidence, and (2) an *à priori* suspicion caused by the connection of the miracles with a reputed revelation. As I have already said,[2] the former of these difficulties

[1] Professor Huxley, *Nineteenth Century*, xxv., p. 189.
[2] Second Lecture, page 20.

has been so fully discussed of late years that it need not detain us. Suffice it to say that the investigations of the most competent scholars have led to this result, that the story of the Christ whom Paul preached corresponded in its main outlines with that which we have received. Thus, if the belief in the divinity and resurrection of Christ were an illusion, it arose in the earliest days of the evolution of the creed, at which time, we may remark, the indirect historic evidence does not indicate the existence of an environment very favourable to its development.

We pass on, then, to the second difficulty: "The connection of occurrences called miraculous with an alleged revelation of itself awakens our suspicions." Undoubtedly we do well to scrutinize carefully the evidence in all such cases. A sceptical attitude is justifiable because testimony is undeniably fallible; the more picturesque aspect of a story is always developed in the telling, and men as a rule not only are credulous, but also have a love of the marvellous. But to refuse belief on no other grounds is as unscientific as to believe simply because the statement is incredible. Suppose we say that we reject the story of Christ's resurrection because men are prone to exaggerate. If we resist too stoutly on this ground, there are passages in the history of science which will not stand a very close scrutiny, and her credit may be found to have suffered from having kept company with astrologers, alchemists, and quacks of various kinds. Suppose we reject the story because there are discrepancies in the minor historic details. If we are going to act on this principle in ordinary history, not very much will survive the trial. On such grounds we should have serious doubts as to the most remarkable events with which this building is connected. The details of the death-scene of Charles I. are even now a subject of dispute;[1] the accounts of his funeral vary so strangely that the burial-place, until the discovery of his body early in the present century, was at least doubtful;[2] but this does not shake our belief in the main facts.

But some say we must disbelieve the Christian story, because alleged miracles are so common in ecclesiastical history. That is to say, we must either reject all or accept all. I might to this make the old retort that the existence of a forgery assumes that of a genuine original, but without pressing this argument,

---

[1] Referring to a controversy then being carried on in the *Times* newspaper, as to whether the block on which the king laid his head were only a few inches in height, or like that which was used at the execution of the Jacobite noblemen on Tower Hill.

[2] The discrepancies of competent historians make this an excellent subject for "Historic Doubts" (see *Halford, Essays*, p. 157).

which I think has a certain weight, I decline to accept the alternative. In science I am frequently called upon to receive, on the authority of others, statements which appear to me very like assertions of the occurrence of miracles; that is, they affirm as facts things which are not in accordance with the laws of nature, so far as I know them. If I refuse credence to some one of these statements, because in this particular case my special knowledge indicates to me that it is more probable testimony should be false than that the miracle should be true, I am not thereby precluded from accepting some other statement—though to me it is equally surprising—which seems to be better substantiated, and more in harmony with analogies already established.

In dealing with an alleged miracle we must not, as I have said, regard the event alone, but also take into consideration the ethical or theological system with which it is connected. Is there no such connection, so that the event is a mere thaumaturgic display, then we may reasonably doubt whether it is in accordance with the mode in which God appears to work. Is the system repugnant to our moral sense, then we are justified in withholding belief. Does the system regard truth as all-important, then fraud is improbable. Is it sober and restrained in statement, then illusion is unlikely. Is the event itself fraught with meaning, essentially didactic, then it is the more likely to have happened, unless revelation be a process in itself incredible.

If, however, it be the Will of God to reveal Himself to man—that is, to disclose to him something more of the ultimate realities than he is able to learn from his environment, which can only lead him to an apprehension of the conditioned; to teach, as does a wise preceptor, sometimes by word of mouth instead of leaving the pupil wholly to lesson-books;—then it seems to me that, as the former is a process different from the latter, the ordinary routine must be varied. Revelation without miracle—using the common phrase —as it seems to me, is no revelation at all. The word "revelation" presupposes that an unusual and unprecedented force comes into play in the world's order; what marvel that novel results should follow in that part which is visible to and appreciable by our ordinary senses? The electric current by which we communicate our thoughts to distant places produces, as it works, physical effects which, to him who is ignorant, are violations and suspensions of the laws of nature. Twice in the world's history, as it has often been pointed out, events have happened which are miraculous to us. These are the beginning of the universe, the creation, as it is called, of matter; and the beginning of life, which, in whatever relation it may stand to the physical forces, cannot be explained as a mere combination of them.

Again, if once we admit the possibility of a revelation, that is, of the disclosure of truths not attainable by our senses, which can only deal with natural objects, are we unreasonable in demanding some sign, some authentication of the message; in expecting some visible indication of the invisible energy, just as the light which glows in the carbon loop of the electric lamp denotes that the invisible current from the unseen battery is passing through it? We cannot accept the terms of the message, taken by itself, as a sufficient proof of its authority. It may be attractive, specious, but after all an *ignis fatuus* to lead me astray into the sloughs of delusion and error. Experience shows that the way of truth is not always the most attractive. I need, therefore, some credentials of another kind, unless I am to remain for long in a condition of great hesitancy and sore perplexity.

These credentials, it seems to me, we have in Christianity, when stripped of the parasitic growth of ecclesiasticism, when reduced to the simple story and simple theology of its earliest age as indicated in the pages of the New Testament. This discloses to us an epoch in the world's history when a force, which we can only view as creative, for a brief period operated with exceptional activity. Granted that each new individual endowed with consciousness of personality is in some sense a creation, there was here a new birth of deeper significance, of more permanent result. Granted that each forerunner in whom the Divine Energy was specially manifested was in some sense an incarnation, here was one in the highest and completest. The birth of Christ and the resurrection of Christ figured and fulfilled the ultimate destiny of man, gave the long-sought answer to the dark enigma of his life, and replaced uncertainty by hope. They enforced the lesson of self-sacrifice, and at the same time demonstrated that the imitation of Christ was not a futile effort; that the way of the Cross, hard and thorny though it is, undoubtedly leads at last to a better land and unclouded happiness. "I am the Resurrection and the Life," said One in Palestine more than eighteen centuries since. If He were only a dreamer or a dream; if the central article of the Christian creed have no other authority than that which can be obtained from the inductive treatment of the objects of sense;—then I tell you frankly that your hope of a future life is indeed a pleasant and a poetic fancy, but it will vanish before the cold logic of physical facts as the glow of the evening sky fades before the darkness of the coming night.

THE PRESENT CONFLICT OF SCIENCE AND THEOLOGY (Boyle Lectures, No. IV.).[1]

"I came forth from the Father, and am come into the world: again I leave the world, and go to the Father."
St. John xvi. 28.

Attempts have been made, more especially of late years, to prove that the section of St. John's Gospel from which these words are quoted is not a record of the actual teaching of Jesus, but a series of imaginary discourses, ascribed to Him by a theologian of a later age. Controversy, as it appears to me, has established at least these results—that the book was already in existence very early in the second century; that its theology is in accord with that of the Apostolic age, though certain points have been treated with unusual fulness; that if we regard its statements, not as the words of Jesus, but only as the metaphysical speculations of some one of His disciples, no trace can be

[1] Preached in the Chapel Royal, Whitehall, on the First Sunday after Trinity, 1890.

found, within the century which followed His death, of the existence of any one who was a thinker at once so profound and so audacious; for surely at that time it would have been deemed audacity—nay, profanity—to fabricate such discourses and make such claims as they involve. Christian literature, if we speak as ordinary critics, begins at an early period to exhibit a marked decadence, as any one may see who will take the trouble to compare the best specimens of the post-Apostolic age with the Scriptures of the New Testament.

It is, then, my present purpose to carry somewhat further the line of argument which I adopted on the last occasion, by pointing out that, as it seems to me, we find, in the history of Christianity and its forerunner Judaism, indications of a revelation. By this I mean, as already explained, a step in the education of man which does not seem to result from the ordinary processes of evolution—which, when regarded from our point of view, appears as a discontinuity, and thus an exception to the general law of continuous operation.

I will only remind you—for it is often forgotten alike by friends and by foes—that in making the following admissions, in conceding very much, as some would say, to the latter, I am very far from granting the conclusions which, in their opinion, are necessary consequences.

1. Continuity of sequence, evolution, development through processes which we call natural (this being only our way of saying that they are familiar), appears to me the rule in this world; the law of nature as it is commonly called. This, however, does not to my mind make it the less the work of God. Our most rigid scientific thinkers enjoin me to recognize in it the operation of an Infinite Energy. So far, then, we are perfectly in accord, only I go further than they, and as I ascribe to this certain characteristics (speaking as a man), I prefer to call it God.

2. I admit that continuity is also the general rule in what we may call the religious education of the world. But I must add that here also, as in nature, the observation of a series of sequences is not equivalent to a discovery of cause. We must not forget the old difference between *How* and *Why*.[1]

3. I admit that a relative element is present in all revelation, because, humanly speaking, I do not see how absolute truth could in any case be imparted to a being conditioned as man, or how even relative

---

[1] *Madam How and Lady Why*, by my late friend Charles Kingsley, is a book for children, but is full of lessons for older folk, as is the case with other like works from the same pen.

truth could germinate and fructify if the seed were dropped on a soil wholly unsuitable. If I may say it without profanity, there is not for God one law in nature and another in revelation. When He would telegraph to man, the message is transmitted along the best conductor that may be found, though a new substance is not created for the occasion.

I make all these admissions, and yet feel justified in declining to accept the conclusions to which they are thought to lead, or the alternatives to which I am supposed to be forced. These, perhaps, I should briefly notice in passing. One of them amounts to this: I must conclude that the Unlimited Cause "took the disguise of a man for the purpose of covenanting with a shepherd chief in Syria."[1] I do not, indeed, admit that this sentence accurately expresses the fact; but, letting that pass, I feel entitled to compliment the critic on his capacity for prescribing to the Infinite His modes of operation. The saying is thoroughly man-like. It is the outcome of a spirit like that which makes small people arrogant with those whom they consider to be socially their inferiors, and leads men to regard with contempt all else that lives on this our globe. "What God hath cleansed, that call not thou common," we might justly retort.

[1] Herbert Spencer, *Ecclesiastical Institutions*, § 588.

Another conclusion to which I am supposed to be forced, is this: That the Infinite Energy, when revealed under the human form, ascribed to Himself limited knowledge, and exhibited a defective moral sense. As already said, I do not expect that the personality—or supposed personality of the messenger—would be lost by absorption; nor can I believe that the message would have been of much use if it had been made to conform to the intellectual requirements and moral status (which may be a fallible standard) of the nineteenth century after Christ.

The third conclusion is this: That if the Christian religion is not of like origin and development with others, it must follow that "a complete simulation of the natural by the supernatural has been deliberately devised to deceive those who examine critically what they are taught; appearances have been arranged for the purpose of misleading sincere inquirers, that they may be eternally damned for seeking the truth."[1] I am aware that the words of many Christians and of certain Churches give some colour to the assumption which this statement involves; but, as I find no valid foundation for it in the authorized formulas of my own Church, and still less in its charter, the sayings of

[1] Idem, § 588, conclusion.

Christ and His Apostles, the noose, into which I am supposed to be inveigled, appears to me no better than a phantom.

We have, then, to inquire whether, admitting the existence in both the Hebrew and the Christian religion, of a process of development in accordance with the laws of continuity and the methods of evolution, we can discover in their histories indications of discontinuities which justify us in recognizing them as revelations.

The most elementary condition of the religious idea appears to be some form of animism, exhibited in shamanism or in fetish-worship. By extension from this—possibly through the idea of the existence of ghosts or through some form of ancestor-worship— we arrive at polytheism, and from this two lines of development seem possible, either to an esoteric pantheism or to henotheism; the latter being the acknowledgment of one divinity, whose status is essentially higher than that of all the rest—the monarchical idea, as we may call it, in theology.

But this is distinct from monotheism, for that repudiates the existence of any other gods, however subordinate in rank.) Monotheism, indeed, has a closer affinity with pantheism, though from this it differs essentially in distinguishing cause from effect, and in ascribing to the First Cause certain qualities which, for want of a better term, we designate personal.

Now, what phenomena are presented to us by the more ancient Hebrew writings? For this inquiry, it is not necessary to enter upon questions as to the possible composite origin or later recensions of the older books of the Bible. It is, I believe, generally admitted that the portions to which I shall refer are of great antiquity. The first of these narrates the early history of the earth and of the human race. In very ancient Chaldean records we find accounts so similar that we can hardly doubt that they are derived from the same original.[1] But between the two versions there is one remarkable difference. The Chaldean legends, as it has been happily expressed, "are saturated with polytheism."[2] From the Hebrew this element has been so thoroughly expurgated that it can only be traced—if, indeed, the recognition be more than fanciful—in the plural word which in certain cases designates God.[3] By whom was this change made? There are but two persons to whom

---

[1] For a convenient account of these, we may refer to the volume on the history of Chaldea, by A. Ragozin, in *The Story of the Nations.*

[2] I heard the phrase used a short time since in an address by the present Bishop of Manchester.

[3] *Elohim.*

we can reasonably attribute it; these are Moses and Abraham. But the relationships of the former were with Egypt, not with Chaldea; so that, apart from other considerations, we conclude that Abraham formed the link between Chaldean and Hebrew tradition; that he expurgated the familiar stories, and illuminated them with a new light. But what enabled him to make this mighty advance in theology, the greatest stride of which we can find any trace in the ancient world? He was surrounded, admittedly, by opposite influences. We are distinctly told—and there is no ground for doubting the statement—that he was the companion and the descendant of polytheists.[1] So far as I know, not a particle of evidence exists that the human race had advanced at that time even so far as henotheism, and from this to monotheism is a long step. Hence, in accordance with the ordinary laws of evolution, the appearance of a monotheist at that epoch of the world's history is an event as improbable as the discovery of the remains of man in a deposit of Miocene age would be in geology. As an evolutionist, I am unable to credit, without the strongest evidence, the alleged occurrence of either the one or the other.

Further, as monotheists, the patriarchs were so far

[1] Josh. xxiv. 2.

in advance of their age that the idea fell on an almost fruitless soil. Their descendants relapsed into henotheism at best, into polytheism at worst. The faith of Abraham must have become almost extinct during the period of bondage in Egypt. Then arose Moses. Brought up at the court of Egypt, he was learned in the wisdom of the Egyptians. After a long exile in the desert, cut off from communication with philosophers or students, associated with nomad tribes, among whom we can hardly deem it possible that a pure monotheism could have survived—if, indeed, it had ever obtained a footing—he makes his mark as a religious reformer not less than as a political leader. Can we regard him, in the former character, as a result of evolutionary processes? Was the idea of which he was the apostle—to use a modern phrase—already in the air? Certainly it was not so in Egypt; there is not a particle of evidence that it was so in Chaldea. Granted that, in another such phrase, he had been already anticipated by Abraham and the fathers of Israel, had not their doctrine been almost overpowered in the struggle for existence by the conceptions then dominant in the national mind? Moses, too, was a man in advance of his age—"born out of due time." For the sake of argument, let us admit the presence of a legendary element in the history of the settlement of the Hebrew race in Palestine; let us concede that, in its present form, it may be somewhat later than the age of Moses; then, I ask, what do I learn, by inductive treatment even of these materials, as to the state of thought among the Hebrews up to—let us say—the days of David? It is this: that monotheism at that period practically had no firm hold upon the nation. The Hebrews at heart were polytheists, only better than the neighbouring tribes in that a vague recollection of primeval tradition at times resulted in a kind of monotheism.

The position occupied by the Hebrew prophets seems to me to have an important significance in this connection. They are not depicted as philosophers, persuading their countrymen to monotheism by arguments. They are not men of culture, representatives of the esoteric thought of a priestly caste; but they come, whence one hardly knows, as critics, and often as opponents, of the very men by whom we should have expected them to have been educated and produced. They proclaim monotheism as a message; they teach it as a system. They are like missionaries of an organization, of which, however, there is no trace; men with a commission, but by whom granted we cannot discover. They have generally small influence, are often persecuted; their doctrine makes little way until Samaria falls before the Assyrian, and Jerusalem before the Chaldean. But if Jewish monotheism were the result simply of an evolutionary process, it ought not to have waged this unequal struggle for existence. It should have been supported throughout, not by the almost spasmodic efforts of rare individual champions, but by the gradually increasing strength of public opinion. Its battle, like a Homeric victory, has been won by the prowess of a hero; Nature's battles are democratic, won by the rank-and-file. Not one of the men who gave the great impulses to Jewish thought can be called a normal product of his age, if we depend solely upon evolutionary processes. These might have produced a Joshua, not a Moses; a Solomon, not a David; a Hezekiah, not an Isaiah.

But it might be argued, of these early days our records are few, our conceptions necessarily vague. Let us turn, then, to an epoch of which we have a fuller knowledge—the beginning of Christianity. Efforts have been made to represent the history of the life of Jesus as little better than a cloud of legend. This attempt is necessary if we start with a disbelief, on *à priori* grounds, in every occurrence which we call miraculous. But the method employed only succeeds in dissipating certain theories as to the nature of revelation, which prove, on examination, to have no valid basis, or in compelling us, if we are consistent, to take up a position of universal scepticism as regards history.

Putting aside for a moment the alleged miracles, how are we to explain the genesis of the doctrine taught by Christ? That there was a preparation for it, that—to use modern phrases—in this or that He had been anticipated, that some ideas were already in the air, I am not concerned to deny; for, as I have said, I believe, as a consistent theist, all development to be by the power of God, and evolution His ordinary mode of working. But I cannot thus explain the phenomena. What are the facts? Jesus was the reputed son of a carpenter in humble circumstances. He had received but little education. He owed nothing to the philosophers of Greece or Rome. He was distinctly hostile, not only to the modes of thought and of instruction which were then dominant in Judaism, but also to its general tendency for at least two centuries previously. There is no evidence that He was influenced by the teaching of Philo. This, indeed, on chronological grounds alone, is highly improbable. Neither can we make that assertion of His disciples, because between their doctrine and this peculiar combination of Hellenistic and rabbinic schools of thought there is at most only an occasional correspondence in terminology, while there is an essential difference in fundamental conceptions.[1]

Jesus also took up a position very different from that of the ordinary reformer. It has little in common with that of such men as Wycliffe or Luther. They confuted the errors of the present by an appeal to the past; Christ, by the enunciation of a new principle of action, though He pointed out that the Law was being obeyed in the letter, but broken in its spirit. They, in short, looked backward; He, forward.

What influences were in His favour? So long as His teaching seemed to foster the national sentiment, it was popular with the people, who chafed under the Roman yoke. But when it became clear that His aim was not political, the multitude left Him to the ecclesiastics, who naturally had been His enemies from the first. He was crucified—He died the death of a detected impostor. His followers admit that they deserted Him. They despaired. Yet, in a short time, these timid fugitives become the brave heralds of a message for the terms of which we look in vain into the speculations of the rabbi or of the philosopher.

The whole history of Christianity is not that of

[1] See Edersheim, *Life and Times of Jesus the Messiah*, bk. i., especially chap. iv.

natural growth alone. Its origin is inexplicable as an evolutionary process. It stands to earlier creeds, even Judaism itself, in a relation resembling that of life to the physical forces in this world's order. It co-operates with, in a sense it absorbs them; yet it is not identical with them. Between the history of Christian and scientific progress there is little in common. In the latter, though advance may be slow, backsliding is rare. Error, once pierced by the spear of truth, is abandoned to the fostering care of the crotchet-monger and the puzzle-head. But Christianity, like Judaism formerly, has to wage a struggle for existence. It seems hardly possible to keep it in its original purity. Dare we say that, even in this nineteenth century, no trace of fetish-worship lingers, no taint of polytheism still infects? Might not Christian Churches even now move St. Paul, could he return to earth, to that plainness of speech which he used to his Galatian converts? It is hardly too much to say that science has developed in accordance with the natural tendencies of the human race, but Christianity—in so far as it has developed—in opposition to them.

Thus while in all progress, in all evolution of religious thought and ethical principles, I discern the guidance of God; while through all the ages past I recognize a light broadening and brightening towards the more perfect day, I find, both in Judaism and in Christianity, processes which may rightly be termed creative, and the very errors of the disciples of the one or the other strengthen the claim of each to an origin not of this world's order.

More than eighteen centuries are past and gone—eighteen centuries, with all their mistakes and all their advances in knowledge—yet the life of Jesus has lost none of its magnetic force, the words of Jesus none of their quickening power. Strange illusion this, if such it be, to have so much vitality that even now each one of us, as life's perplexities increase, as its sad lessons are enforced by sorrowful experience, as the evening shadows begin to lengthen and the sands run low in his appointed measure of time, feels that he can only re-echo the question of Christ's first disciples, "Lord, to whom shall we go? Thou hast the words of eternal life."

THE PRESENT CONFLICT OF SCIENCE AND THEOLOGY (BOYLE LECTURES, No. V.).[1]

"I delight in the Law of God after the inward man: but I see another law in my members, warring against the law of my mind, and bringing me into captivity to the law of sin which is in my members."—ROM. VII. 22, 23.

I HAVE endeavoured, in previous lectures, to show that there is no necessary conflict between the conclusions of science and the belief in a revelation; that we must look to the latter for all knowledge of God which is other than relative; but that we find nothing in the former to make an expectation of His guidance unreasonable; that, in short, the conflict of theology and science arises from partial and one-sided views on the part of their advocates.

If, then, we are fully persuaded that the Author of Nature and of Revelation is One and the same, we are more than justified in the hope that the hieroglyphs which we seek to decipher on the pages of the one

[1] Preached in the Chapel Royal, Whitehall, on the Second Sunday after Trinity, 1890.

volume may throw light on the interpretations of sayings which, in the other, are often beyond our present comprehension. I purpose, then, in the remaining lectures of this course, to inquire whether these imaginary adversaries may not be sometimes mutually helpful, and especially whether some explanation of difficulties, which undoubtedly exist in theology, may not be found in science, that is, in the inductive treatment of the phenomena of Nature. To cover so wide a field is obviously impossible, so that I shall restrict myself to certain instances. One of these, perhaps the most saddening, is indicated by the words which I have read. They speak of a conflict which all of us know too well. They represent the individual man as a battle-field of two opposing forces. The passage from which they come, as all admit, is hard to interpret; but this is due rather to the nature of the subject than to the fault of the writer. Do the words, let us ask, become more easy to comprehend when regarded from the standpoint to which we are led by scientific induction?

There is a dark shadow in Christianity, there is a grave difficulty in every ethical system, there is a discord in the harmony of Nature, which has perplexed alike philosopher and saint. This is the existence of evil. Whence did it arise? how did it come? Can science help us in solving the problem?[1] Two modes of eluding the difficulty should, perhaps, be mentioned in order to avoid misapprehension, though they need not be discussed, because it is generally admitted that neither can be regarded as satisfactory. These are: To assert that evil is only good in another form, which practically is a denial of its existence; or that there is an eternal principle of evil antagonistic to that of good—the well-known dualism of some Eastern philosophers.

The position adopted by most theists, and all or almost all Christians, may be concisely—if rather baldly—stated as follows: "God is perfect goodness. God is Creator and Author of all things. Evil is present among them, at any rate in this world." If this be so, one conclusion only seems possible, from which, however, we naturally shrink. Even if we ascribe, as is generally done, the presence of evil in this world to the action of a particular person, this obviously affords no explanation of its origin; and, however true the opinion may be, it leaves a number of difficult questions quite untouched.

Let us turn to the book of Nature, and see what light

---

[1] The treatment of the question is necessarily brief. A fuller discussion will be found in a discourse, earlier in date, but printed at the end of the present volume.

it can throw on this dark place in theology. We must be careful, at the outset, to avoid a common confusion of thought. This arises from the double sense in which the word "evil" is ordinarily employed, and the consequent failure to distinguish between the physical and the moral. Doubtless it is not always easy, owing to the continuity which reigns in Nature, to draw a sharp line between the two provinces. Moral evil may sometimes stand in close connection with physical environment, and thus give rise to difficulties in practice, but in thought they not only are perfectly separable, but also must be separated.

To physical evil, as we sometimes call it—to pain, disease, death—I make no reference. They were not imported into the world, as has been sometimes imagined, at a late epoch in its history. They are practically as old as sensation; all but as old as life. I do not say that a world free from them is a thing inconceivable, but it would not be this world. So long as matter retains the properties which it now possesses; so long as the physical forces continue; so long as the relation of life, whatever it be, to organism be the same;—so long must living beings, in their season, sicken, suffer, and die. We may wish this otherwise, but it is inevitable, and we must console ourselves by remembering that pain, a mode of sensation in all organized beings, has obviously been the stimulus which has been a great factor—if it has been nothing more—in their evolution.

But moral evil seems to stand in a different relation to living beings. It is less difficult to imagine a system like the present into which it did not enter. But in inquiring its origin, we may find our way rendered easier by endeavouring to ascertain what is the true nature of evil. How shall we define it? There is a general idea that evil is a positive; more careful consideration will, I think, show that this is erroneous. Its relation to good may be compared with that of darkness to light. The latter is a positive, for it is a mode of motion; the former is a negative—no-motion, and so a relative to light. All evil presupposes goodness, from which it is a deviation; all wrong presupposes right. We call an action right or wrong because we try it by a standard. Obviously, if there were no such standard, the comparison could not be made. It follows, therefore, that the moral significance of the action is relative to the standard. Hence if the latter be changed, the former also changes, and that which would be right under one condition of things, might become wrong under another. We may illustrate this by the analogy which I have just employed. If we were to step from the full sunlight into a shaded room, this to us would be dark, while to those who had been there for long, the light would suffice for their purposes. Yet that which we had been enjoying, that, which made their light to us relatively darkness, to them for a time would be blinding by its excess.

Now, what can we learn from the analogy of Nature? Its great stone-book exhibits a gradual progress in development among living beings: forms more specialized, that is, more perfectly in adaptation to their environment, replacing those which are more generalized. Whatever may be the precise explanation of the phenomena, we cannot deny that even the animal world has been subjected to a process which may be termed, in a large sense of the word, an education, and the increase of our knowledge only deepens the conviction that this process, as a rule, is continuous, even if there be exceptional discontinuities.

Another point is no less certain, namely, that, whatever be the explanation, man, considered simply as an organized being, is indistinguishable from other animals. That he may be something more than an animal I have no intention of denying, but I affirm that, if we restrict ourselves to the methods of investigation which are commonly regarded as scientific, we cannot draw a hard-and-fast line between him and the rest of the animal world. Every attempt to do this has been a failure, and we must admit—whatever difficulties may seem to threaten—that any differences which can be discovered are in degree, not in kind. Our sensations are similar, our emotions are due to like causes. It does not, however, follow that the actions in which these result are identical in moral value, simply because they have the same physical cause. If an animal acts in accordance with its natural impulses, we do not consider it to have done wrong, even though this leads us to kill it as hurtful or obnoxious to us. We may sometimes apply to an animal such terms as "malicious," "murderous," "lustful;" yet we are fully aware that these epithets, with all others imputing moral qualities, are only used in a figurative sense. But in a man, a certain course of action becomes wrong because something—what this may be is immaterial for our present purpose; call it, if you will, an inherited instinct—has told him that in such cases he must resist his natural impulses. When, for instance, I am hungry, the sensation has a history altogether similar in myself and in a wild animal; its purpose, if I may so call it, is the development and preservation of the body. The animal takes the first suitable food it finds, and thereby does right, because it knows no other duty than the maintenance of its

F

life and strength; but, in adopting the same course, I may do wrong, because I have learnt that, under certain circumstances, it is my duty to suffer rather than to gratify my desires.

Do we not, even in ourselves, recognize that the moral value of actions changes with circumstances? To take an obvious example: Something which is the property of another attracts the eye of a little child. The hand is instinctively stretched out to take it. The action itself is not regarded as wrong, though, for purposes of education, it may be checked, even in an infant; but as time goes on, and ideas of property are acquired, the "taking" becomes "stealing" or "robbing," and the action a sin. Yet then it is condemned by the moralist more severely in proportion to the clearness with which these ideas have been impressed upon and presumably recognized by the offender. But it might be said this does away with any absolute standard, and makes the individual the measure of the moral value of his actions. Certainly it does; but that does not lighten individual responsibility. For if a man has lost all sense of this by continuous and deliberate wrong-doing, he must bear the burden of having subjected himself to the process. Nor does it interfere with the administration of law, because that necessarily adopts rough-and-ready methods of classification, and yet it now recognizes extenuating circumstances. We even go so far as to admit that some persons are not responsible for their actions; but this does not give rise to any serious difficulty. In such a case the onus of proving non-responsibility is thrown on the individual, and into minor distinctions the law in many cases cannot enter, because its penalties are measured, not so much by absolute justice to the individual, as by the requirements of justice for the society.

But on this point it is needless to enlarge further, because I think few persons, after a little consideration, will refuse to admit that the moral value of an action depends upon the ethical position of the doer—that, in the Apostle's words, where there is no law there can be no sin.[1]

Goodness, then, in any race of beings, would consist in perfect conformity with their environment, using the term in a very wide sense. Let us suppose this to be in some way or other modified—restricting ourselves to its ethical side. Let us suppose that by some means an impulse is received towards a higher stage of existence; that, for purposes of education, something which before was perfectly legitimate is forbidden, or some course of conduct is enjoined which

[1] See Rom. v.-vii.

was previously without precedent; that, in fact, a new ideal of duty is originated—a new standard is set up. Conflict thus arises between the old habit and the new impulse. The former—the principle of heredity, as we may call it—urges to inaction or to one course of conduct; the latter, the new motive force, to another. We must assume the existence of a power of selection, of choice, of free-will; for without this, moral responsibility cannot exist. At once that which we call evil becomes possible—potentially it comes into existence. To follow the new course is right; to abide in the old, though formerly it was right, has become wrong. Hence evil is inseparable in thought from every system of progressive moral development, provided that the individuals be capable of exercising choice. If one of them, instead of obeying the onward and upward impulse, elects to continue in his former condition, the preference for the *status quo*, as we may call it, though it formerly constituted good, has now become evil.

Suppose, as an illustration, that the ethical state of a group of living creatures is represented by the movements of a number of points, and that goodness is signified by these taking place in a particular plane. Suppose also that—owing to some previous influence, the nature of which is immaterial—

they take place in this plane: we have thus a permanent goodness. But now suppose the plane to become a surface curving upwards (which introduces the idea of a discontinuity), while at the same time the points are influenced by a force which of itself would cause them to move in a new direction. At once there is a conflict between this and the tendency of movement already acquired. Some modification must result. It may be that the new attraction will retain the points in the new surface, but it may be that the acquired tendency will cause them to deviate from it. By so doing, even by remaining in the original plane, they assume a position which is relatively evil, though, of course, to make it really this, as we interpret the word, we must conceive the points endowed with a power of choice, whether they will or will not yield to the new influence.

It follows, then, that evil has its origin, not in a departure from an ideal perfection, but in a refusal to obey the impulses tending towards an ideal perfection. While we cannot deny the possibility of its existence in beings other than ourselves, we can only—so long as we restrict ourselves to this world, of which alone our perceptions can take cognizance—affirm its existence in our own race, because we cannot prove that a sense of moral responsibility exists in any other.

Still analogous conditions may be found elsewhere among living creatures; for obviously evil is inconceivable in the inorganic world. In the great stone-book of Nature we read the history of many a race which has proved incapable of adapting itself to a changed environment, and has paid the penalty by deterioration, suffering, and ultimate extinction; but we alone, so far as we know, can deliberately resist the great evolutionary purpose, can be as Gods, knowing good and evil, and choose the latter—that is to say, with a power of recognizing the upward tendency, can deliberately prefer to continue in the lower condition.

Can we advance any further in our inquiry? We learn from science that, structurally, man cannot be differentiated from the rest of the animal world. An inductive treatment of the whole body of facts which can be collected in relation to his history, socially as well as physiologically, may indeed justify the suspicion that he is something more; but it can go no further, and for any actual knowledge we must be indebted to revelation. This tells us that in man's composite nature there is a spiritual factor, but gives us no definite information—why should it?—as to the bodily factor. It soon becomes evident that the statements in Scripture concerning the latter cannot be pressed in a sense strictly literal, but must be regarded as figurative or expressive of relative rather than actual knowledge. If we refuse to admit this, we have no other choice than to repudiate the evidence of our senses and the use of our reason, and blindly to submit to some authority; though without these I do not see how we can test its claims to be obeyed.

As I suppose we should be unwilling to adopt the latter course, we may legitimately seek information from the results of scientific study. These, in the opinion of some well qualified to speak, lead to the conclusion that, whatever discontinuity there may be in the history of man as a living soul, to use the ordinary phrase, he also is an example of the great law of continuity, and that his bodily part is strictly animal in its origin; that just as there is in the embryonic individual a process of development from the lowest to the highest type of organism, so it was in the embryonic race. Thus the "body of this death," as the Apostle so truly calls it, is our inheritance from the animal world; our passions are the survival of instincts transmitted from an animal ancestry, which the Spirit now calls upon us to check and to mortify. It is this new birth of the race, this impulse to

> "Move upward, working out the beast,
> And let the ape and tiger die." [1]

---

[1] Tennyson, *In Memoriam*, cxviii.

which has made these instincts evil, has made evil possible—has been, in a sense, the beginning of sin.

This idea as to the descent of the bodily part of man from an animal ancestry cannot, it is true, be reckoned among the conclusions of science, but it is an hypothesis, the evidence for which has certainly become stronger with the progress of knowledge. It is one which, I am well aware, has greatly startled and shocked many earnest Christians. It has been supposed to involve a denial of moral responsibility and of the existence of a spiritual constituent in human nature. What I have said has, I hope, made it evident that this opinion as to the origin of the human race is perfectly consistent with the admission of both the one and the other. To deny the former, indeed, would, as it appears to me, be difficult for a scientific man; for it seems to meet with general acceptance as the result of an inductive treatment of facts, quite apart from any statements of a supposed revelation. To deny the latter would obviously be as impossible as to affirm it, as a result of scientific processes, because these could not take us beyond a probability for it or against it.

But some difficulties, which admittedly exist, seem to be explained by this idea, while those which it is supposed to create have no existence if once we recognize the facts—as they appear to me—that revelation is progressive and in certain cases relative; that its end is not to tell us the solution of problems which we may discover for ourselves, sooner or later, by patient labour, but to raise a veil which our hands could not have moved or even touched, to lead us onwards and upwards through this world's drifting clouds and perplexing mists towards that eternal light on which mortal eyes cannot gaze, to that boundless love which has deemed our frail and faulty natures worth lifting upwards and preserving for some work, in æons yet to come, in spheres to us as yet unknown, where sin cannot enter, because the "body of this death" will have crumbled to its harmless elements of inorganic and consequently innocent matter, because the will of the redeemed soul will be in perfect conformity with the will of God, and the body which then shall be, if one with this in its vital principle, will be free from the law of heredity, for there will be no continuity of corporeal organism. Such "is the resurrection of the dead. It is sown in corruption; it is raised in incorruption: it is sown in dishonour; it is raised in glory: it is sown in weakness; it is raised in power: it is sown a natural body; it is raised a spiritual body."

THE PRESENT CONFLICT OF SCIENCE AND THEOLOGY (BOYLE LECTURES, NO. VI.).[1]

> "The Lord passed by before him, and proclaimed, The Lord, The Lord God, merciful, and gracious, long-suffering, and abundant in goodness and truth, keeping mercy for thousands, forgiving iniquity and transgression and sin, and that will by no means clear the guilty; visiting the iniquity of the fathers upon the children, and upon the children's children."—EXOD. xxxiv. 6, 7.

ARE the clauses of this remarkable passage contradictory? Do they ascribe to God attributes which cannot be reconciled? That is not an uncommon opinion. Perhaps, however, they may be softened or explained away in the fuller light of the Gospel dispensation. But Christianity is often supposed to be yet more uncompromising. It teaches, in the opinion of one of its critics, "the visiting on Adam's descendants, through hundreds of generations, dreadful penalties for a small transgression which they did not commit; the damning of all men who do not avail

[1] Preached in the Chapel Royal, Whitehall, on the Fourth Sunday after Trinity, 1890.

themselves of an alleged mode of obtaining forgiveness, which most men have never heard of; and the effecting a reconciliation by sacrificing a Son who was perfectly innocent, to satisfy the assumed necessity for a propitiatory victim."[1] This, I say, is considered to be a fair statement of its doctrine. To myself it appears to be a caricature, but I must sorrowfully admit that, if we accept the dogmas of some Churches and the opinions of not a few individuals as a fair statement of the teaching of the New Testament, this picture can hardly be called exaggerated.

Under these circumstances, let us endeavour to ascertain whether the Book of Nature throws any light on this dark place in the Book of Revelation, when it states that God will by no means clear the guilty, but will visit iniquity even upon their descendants. For my present purpose, I must exclude one topic—that of the Atonement—mentioned in the passage which I have just quoted, because it would require a much fuller consideration than it could possibly receive within my present limits, and because I do not hesitate to assert that the clause relating to it is a parody, not, indeed, without some justification, but still a parody of the Christian doctrine as it may be inferred from Scripture.

[1] Herbert Spencer, *Ecclesiastical Institutions*, § 658.

What, then, are we taught there in regard to the remainder of these questions? If we lay aside a theological terminology, and any discussion of the modes, if one may so call them, in which Divine grace —as it appears to the Christian—operates upon the soul of man, it amounts, I think, to this, that our life here on earth is a state of trial; that its issues are eternal,—the goals are life and death; that sin or error brings its punishment, the effects of which reach further than the original wrong-doer. We are told, in short, that life is a conflict, sometimes apparently against heavy odds, where success is uncertain and failure more than possible.

This is held to be hard measure. Be it so or not, let us see how far it accords with the analogy of Nature. What do we learn from this? It discloses four great laws by which all life is governed. These are: first, the law of trial—the conflict with the environment, the struggle for existence against the forces of Nature and the other forms of life, in which, as the conditions of the warfare change, so must the tactics of the combatant be correspondingly altered. The second is the law of inheritance—the principle of heredity, as it is often called. Each generation receives from its ancestry both good and ill, adaptabilities and opponencies to its environment; it is heir to the characteristics, physical and mental, of its progenitors, alike to their strength and their weakness. The third is the law of reward—we call it in science "the survival of the fittest." "To him that overcometh," if we may venture to use the words in a lower sense, "I will give a crown of life," is the law of Nature as well as of grace. The fourth is the law of doom. "Woe to the conquered!" is the inscription graven deep on the crags of the earth. Nature is inexorable; she condones no failure, remits no penalty. The rocks are full of the records of long-vanished races, which have lived their day, fought their fight, and perished in the struggle, to give place to higher and more capable organizations. Here, again, a phrase from revelation may be applied to Nature, though in a lower sense; her doom is this: "The soul that sinneth, it shall die."

Such are the lessons of Nature. Is the teaching of Christianity—divested of technicalities—so very different? It amounts to this: Cause and consequence stand in their invariable and unalterable relation. Before you—it seems to tell us—are two paths, the one straight and narrow, on which the Spirit is guide, of which the goal is life; the other, broad and easy, on which the animal nature leads, of which the goal is destruction. Surely, though the circumstances be different, the principle is the same, and we cannot affirm that there is one rule in Nature, another in Grace.

But, you may reply, "The words which have been read offend us most in this respect, that they proclaim unhesitatingly that the innocent shall suffer for the guilty, and this is repugnant to our sense of justice."

But, I may ask, is there anything in this rule exceptional, abnormal, unprecedented? The innocent suffer for the guilty! How can it be otherwise? When do they not suffer? Can a man squander his property, whether through sin or through unwisdom, without consequential injury to those who are dependent on him? Can he ruin his health by vicious living, without giving cause to every child born of his body to curse his father's sins? Have you never heard of congenital diseases, of ancestral taints of blood, of hereditary phthisis, scrofula, insanity, and the like? Not a day passes but thousands of children are born into this world, doomed by parental vice to a crippled existence or to a premature grave.[1]

Again, consider the case of a nation. This is a true saying, though it be not of Christian origin: "The princes play the fool; the people pay the penalty."[2]

---

[1] If proof of this statement be needed, I may refer to such a work as that on *Syphilis and the Nervous System* (*Lettsomian Lectures*), by Dr. W. R. Gowers, F.R.S. See *Lancet*, 1889, vol. i. p. 63, etc.

[2] "Quicquid delirant reges, plectuntur Achivi," Hor., 1 *Ep.* 2. 14.

It may be altered for a democracy without loss of accuracy: for "princes," read "majority;" for "people," read "minority." This law is writ large on the pages of history. Greek, Jew, Roman, all in their turn have suffered for national crime, national vice, and national folly. The history of modern Europe repeats the same lesson; it proclaims the operation of the eternal and inevitable laws of God, that words, if they do not proceed from His mouth, fail to sustain the life of man; that self-indulgence, whatever form it takes, cannot be substituted for duty as a guiding principle, nor molluscous sentimentality for the plain rule of the Decalogue; that the vices of an aristocracy work a heavy retribution, and the "fool-fury" of democracy brings a yet worse ruin. Many a time has this proverb come true in the past, many a time will it come true in the future, let England be sure of that: "The fathers have eaten sour grapes"—no doubt to their own sorrow—"and the children's teeth are set on edge."[1]

It might be possible to imagine an order of things in which each individual bore only his own burden; but this Utopia would not present the slightest resemblance to the present world, for from it we must abstract every idea of parentage, relationship, and

[1] Ezek. xviii. 2.

mutuality. Each individual in it must be self-complete, self-centred, and independently originated. But the interdependence of the human race, and of all others that we know, is a fact as essential to the world's order as gravitation itself, and is no more capable of being excluded from it. After all, viewing the question broadly, is it so unjust that we should be heirs to our forefathers' losses as well as to their gains? If a man leaves you his property, you cannot repudiate his liabilities!

"But"—I think I can hear our critic urge—"do you admit that men will be damned to eternity for not availing themselves of a mode of obtaining forgiveness of which they have never heard?" I admit no more than this truism, that if I have never heard of Christ, I cannot be saved by the knowledge of Him, and that consequences must follow causes; but beyond this I decline to go; for to express an opinion upon a case, the circumstances of which I have no means of ascertaining, would be an unscientific proceeding. But inasmuch as even man recognizes readily the difference between a deed done with full knowledge of its wrongfulness, and the same done in ignorance, and punishes, if he does it in the latter case, in the hope of educating either the individual or the society, I find no difficulty in believing that the all-knowing Lord of earth and heaven will not be fettered by the imperfect legal forms of human procedure, but will emphatically do what is right. I trust Him, in Whom justice and love are alike perfect; and should I presume to ask, "Lord, and how shall this man fare?" I seem to hear Him answer, "What is that to thee? Follow thou Me."

An objection, however, may be made to the analogy for which I have sought in Nature. This analogy, it is urged, is misleading; for the consequences in the natural order are temporal, while in the spiritual order they are eternal. The objection is less valid than it seems. What consequences are not eternal? Can I, can you, undo that which has been done? No; that—I say it with all reverence—is beyond the power of God Himself. I may remedy, He may remedy, the mistake. The hurt, the fall, through His loving-kindness, may be made to work with all things together for good. The battle lost, by the help of the great Commander may be turned into a battle won;[1] but not seldom the defeat is in the temporal order, the victory in the spiritual. There are many things in this life—failures, losses, sorrows, sins, which, however they may be softened by lapse

[1] The allusion, of course, is to the remark of Desaix to Napoleon at Marengo.

of time, repaired or alleviated by future gains or joys, can never be set right.

Consider an instance, trite though it be. The "desire of our eyes may be taken from us with a stroke"—be this friend, or child, or partner of life. God may by this grief draw us nearer to Him; but henceforth a shadow darkens our path in life where once there was unclouded brightness; there is an aching void where once there was helpful companionship.

To take another instance. Suppose that health has been lost—say from vicious living. Can this be restored by any repentance? God may so dispose the allotted path of inevitable suffering as to find a use even for the consequences of our evil deeds; man may so learn the bitter lesson from the wages of sin as to rise on stepping-stones of his dead self to higher things; but even if, in a certain sense, the crooked may be made straight, that which the cankerworm hath eaten cannot be recovered—the lost limb, so to say, cannot be restored.

But on this topic I need not enlarge. Unless we suppose that a miracle be wrought, the consequences of our actions are eternal. Happy the man whose memory is not haunted by more than one golden cloud-palace of the "might have been"!

But I may still be charged with eluding the issue. I declare, it may be urged, eternal suffering to be the penalty of sin. As this is a subject on which by my own powers I can know nothing, I restrict myself to the words of revelation. But these I accept in what appears to be their plain natural sense, into which I decline to read meanings, however popular and prevalent they may be, when I can discover for them no authority which is more than human. In revelation I am told that eternal life is the gift of God to man, and consists in the knowledge of Him and of Jesus Christ, Whom He sent into the world; that the punishment of sin is sure, and can only be averted, if indeed it can wholly be averted, by repentance; and that the ways of the sinner conduct him, not to eternal life, but to eternal death. This I fully believe; this appears to me in harmony with the analogy of nature. The consideration of how far it corresponds with our critic's assumption, or accords with popular ideas, is an inquiry too long for the present occasion, and immaterial for our immediate purpose. Enough that I believe in retribution, since I believe in justice.[1]

To conclude. Suppose we grant that the Gospel proclaims a hard message when it says, " Sin, and you

---

[1] This subject is noticed, rather more fully, in another sermon in this volume (No. IX.).

shall suffer; sin, and you will find you have hatched a brood of ugly facts, which no smooth words will deprive of vitality. Like young snakes, they slip away among the herbage, and you cannot allure them back to be killed, charm you never so wisely! 'Many are called, but few chosen;' 'The wages of sin is death.'" Is that so hard a message? Are you offended that this is in the Gospel, which the God of love Himself proclaimed? Nature's message is in identical terms, and differs only in this, that its tones are a thousandfold more hopeless. She knows neither ruth nor pity. On her course she goes. Her path is like that of some vast machine, beneath whose wheels, as they roll onwards, myriad, myriad sufferers are crushed, from whose walls the darts of death fly forth, at random as it seems, to smite their helpless victims in the terror-stricken crowd. Nature merciful! Why, in comparison with her, the granite rock is soft, the tiger is an emblem of tenderness.

She points to no Utopia; she offers neither pardon nor redress behind the veil; she declares not only the inevitable supremacy of law, but also, it would seem, the wantonness of cruel chance. This is all the comfort she can give—if I have understood her voice aright: "After that you have suffered, I promise you extinction. I can no more. Do you say you had better never have been born? Perhaps so; I cannot help that."

Suppose, then, we grant that the path which revelation indicates may seem sometimes dark with gloomy shadows, this at least we may claim, that it is bright as with the perfect day in comparison with that which Nature shows. Each may be beset with sorrow and suffering, but the "way of the Cross" leads at length to the peace of heaven and the undimmed gladness of eternal life; the way of Nature can offer no better reward than extinction, no other peace than that of annihilation.

THE PRESENT CONFLICT OF SCIENCE AND THEOLOGY (BOYLE LECTURES, No. VII.).[1]

"Be not ignorant of this one thing, that one day is with the Lord as a thousand years, and a thousand years as one day. The Lord is not slack concerning His promise, as some men count slackness."—2 PET. III. 8, 9.

"ALL things come alike to all: there is one event to the righteous and to the wicked." This, many would tell us, is the sole inference which can be drawn from facts, whether they be those of Nature or of history; it is the one conclusion to which scientific methods of thought must lead. 'Your dream of immortality,' men say; 'your hopes of a continued personal life are founded upon a series of alleged events which have no warrant in history, other than the illusions of some excitable and credulous disciples. We see, in the evolution of the earth and of its tenants, power, but not purpose; energy, but not God.'

"The life of man is as the flowers of the field."

[1] Preached at the Chapel Royal, Whitehall, on the Fifth Sunday after Trinity, 1890.

These, in their season, put forth bud and blossom. They dapple the meadows, they spangle the forest, they kindle the moorland into a glow of colour, but, like the sunset flush, they fade away, less transient than it in this alone, that they have helped in perpetuating the race. "You think," men say, "that the Gospel of Christ brings you a message of hope; but how far is that substantiated by facts?" Very little, if we may trust appearances. "It is nineteen centuries," they continue, "since that Gospel was preached, and what real influence has it obtained in the world? That is enough to show what a futility your prayer, 'Thy kingdom come,' has proved. The failure of Christianity is its condemnation; for it does not satisfy the most convincing of all tests, that of experiment."

"The time is long; the work is without a purpose." Let us, then, see whether the analogy of Nature can give us any help in this perplexity; whether the same criticism, the same complaint, might not have been made by overhasty onlookers full often in the past, and what answer it has received from the logic of facts in the process of the ages. If we grant that change is slow, does Nature justify us in adding, "but it is also sure"? In our investigation of her ways, we must not expect to discover any message of hope for the individual; for him, as it seems to me, she has ever but cold comfort. Something, however, would be gained if we succeeded in obtaining only thus much for our encouragement, that our labour in this world is not a mere making of ropes of sand, so that, whether we have our wages or not, it is better to work than to sit still with folded hands.

It is, indeed, possible that occasionally in the past teleological arguments may have been pressed too far; but we are in danger of undervaluing them at the present time. Nature and History alike bear witness, as it seems to me, to "an increasing purpose." The phenomena of this earth's evolution can hardly be understood except as a manifestation of Mind; and their evidence, positive and negative alike, appear to warrant the inference that, besides purpose, there may be love.

They teach also, it seems to me, another lesson—it is that of patience; they utter a warning—it is against a hasty judgment. "Why," we are tempted to ask, "if Christianity is from God, has it not triumphed? Why does He delay so long to reveal Himself and to help His servants?"

This question we cannot pretend to answer. But we can at least reply that it is what the analogy of Nature would lead us to expect. For that lesson we have to thank science. Once we thought that this world, but a very few thousand years ago, came into sudden existence, as at the waving of an enchanter's wand. Now we have learnt that through millions of years it has been slowly changing from nebula to solid, from incandescent orb to the fit abode of living creatures. Glance at epochs in its history, if it be but for a moment, to convince yourselves that this is true. Millions of years ago—how many we cannot tell—long after the earth's glowing crust had cooled, and the water had gathered in the ocean-depths, the scene differed strangely from that which our eyes now behold. Let us imagine ourselves led, by some immortal guide, as in a vision of poet or prophet, along the "corridors of time." What pictures do we see? There is the earth, warmed by the sun, moistened by the rain; the surf beats on the rock-bound coast; the streams leap down the mountain-side; the rhythmic processes of the physical forces are the same as now. But except from these, there is no other sound. The silence is unbroken by the cry of beast or note of bird. The world is a waste, one vast desert of herbless land and lifeless sea. To what profit is this globe, this monstrous orb of rock, which whirls its useless way through space? So we might well have asked. But wait and see. Let millions of years pass, and again regard the earth. Herbage clothes the soil, trees rise on high, the waters teem with life, the land has its creatures. Yet how strange are all these! "Plants and animals," the voice of science might say, "are alike lowly in organization. The trees are little better than overgrown reeds and club-mosses; the animals at best do not rise above magnified toads." Look also at those miasmatic swamps, so dismal to our eyes. Is this all that the Divine Energy can effect? "Well," our guide might reply, "but for this rank vegetation, these swamps which you despise, a certain coming race, about which you do know a very little, would find itself without its coal-fields, and thus be deprived of a potent factor in its course of progress."

Years roll on in their countless thousands as you watch the changeful vision of life displayed upon the surface of the globe, and at every and any epoch you might ask the same question: Why? For what purpose? Wherefore this delay? Millions of years were spent in making the world; millions of years in preparation for a being who, whatever his destiny, can at any rate appreciate the marvels by which he is surrounded, can rise above the things of sense, and, by the use of reason, search after the unknown and even grope after the unknowable.

Of all these countless years, of all these endless

changes, man—we ourselves, we, the lords of creation, have been the outcome. Life's first germ on this earth's surface, whenever and whatever it may have been, in the dim distance of those unnumbered years, was in a sense the first germ of ourselves; its varied history does but record the phases in that long period of gestation which has ended in the birth of the human race. "How slow!" we might have exclaimed again and again. Yes, but how sure! "How fruitless!" This might have been again and again our verdict. Yes; everything seems useless till time teaches you its utility.

I claim, then, that for the race—I do not speak of the individual—the earth's history tells its tale of purpose, not of the blind working of physical forces; of purpose, which, if you will not call it beneficent, has, at any rate, had progress for its result so uniformly as to justify us in regarding it as tending to that end.

Once more. Look back on the history of the human race; for man also is a unit in the great and complex scheme of Nature. Again I say that this deprives us, more completely than heretofore, of any ground for expecting rapid change or precipitate action. Once we supposed that man's history began some six thousand years ago. Nay, that practically it could not be dated so far back; for the race, not much more than four thousand years since, was reduced to a single family—by whom, as we believed, "the whole earth was overspread." What has science declared to us? We can now perceive the dawn of history in ages which once seemed hopelessly dark. Our horizon has been widened, the date of the genesis of the human race—be that what it may—recedes into a dim and distant past. For we know not how many thousand years, races of men have come and gone on the face of this earth. Even in our own island—then a part of the continent—savage tribes, like those which linger on the Greenland coasts, once shaped the rough flints into rude tools, and hunted, upon its ice-bound shores, wild beasts which have since vanished from the face of the globe.

So creation's story runs; so the tale of man's earlier days is told. We now measure its progress by millenniums rather than by centuries; his history by centuries rather than by years. "The time is long; the work is slow." True; but something seems to come of it which justifies us in doubting whether there is not That behind phenomena which is more than mere Force, more than undirected Energy. This, at least, I think, our knowledge of the history of the earth and of man now warrants us in asserting—that at every epoch in the past, the present has been occupied in preparing what has proved to be a legacy for the future. There fell long since in the depths of oceans now vanished from sight, as there falls still into like depths,[1] one ceaseless shower of the dead shells of tiny organisms which float like a living cloud beneath the waves, and by that shower were built up the white masses of the chalk which lies buried deep beneath our feet, and forms the hills to north and south of this river-valley. These and many another organism lived and died to sow the dust of continents to be. Such has been the law which has reigned on this our earth. What wonder, then, if we find the like in the development of man? Take history—take its facts apart from any connection with religious ideas, and what do they tell us? That there has been a slow change from barbarism to civilization, a slow growth of the moral faculties. If we disbelieve a revelation, we cannot deny an evolution; if we believe in revelation, we must admit an increase in man's capacity for receiving it.

[1] Referring to the Foraminifera, especially the genus *Globigerina*, which is as abundant in parts of the Atlantic as it must have been in the waters under which the chalk of England and North-Western France was deposited. There has been some controversy as to the depth at which it ceases to live, but the evidence seems in favour of its habitat being in a zone from the surface down to a depth of a very few hundred fathoms.

Progress, it is true, has not always been continuous. There has been ebb and flow, like that seen in the ocean-waters when the tide is rising upon the beach. If we fix our eyes too exclusively upon any single epoch, we might often deem that its lesson was of deterioration, not of progress; of decay, not of growth. Now and again darkness seems closing over the earth, and truth flickers above the wild waste like some solitary beacon-light, which the winds threaten to extinguish. Now the last days seem to be at hand, as a civilized race becomes effete, and is swept away by the inroads of more vigorous barbarians. The work of centuries is in danger of being undone in a single generation. The Jew, with all his faults, saw spiritual truths more clearly than the Chaldean, yet Jerusalem goes down before the might of Babylon; the vast and highly organized fabric of the Roman empire totters and falls, even when it has been conquered by the Cross of Christ, before the irresistible flood of barbarian and heathen invaders. Again and again the inevitable rule is exemplified that all things alike wax old, and in their turn decay. But still each nation, as it perishes, leaves to the future some legacy of good. The Greek bequeathed his philosophy; the Roman, his system of law and his example of voluntary discipline; the Jew, his spiritual insight and the all-absorbing intensity of his faith, for which he would even dare to die. The Teuton has set forth the lesson of chastity. The "very perfect knight" of the Middle Ages has made himself a mirror of chivalry. Each, and all, in their turn, have left to us the example of their virtues, the warning of their failures. They have laboured and passed away, and we have entered into their labours. Do we now complain that the time is long; that no purpose can be discovered in the seeming confusion of our life on earth? There is not an impatient word which we can utter, which might not have been said a thousand times over in the past— which probably has been said; for every age is prone to consider itself as the last epoch in the world's history. That after it will come the deluge, in one sense or another of the phrase, is the illusion common to every generation. We who are now living are not exempt from it; tacitly we assume that these are the last times. Those who incline to optimism boast of the triumphs of civilization; they bid us admire this great Babylon, that man has builded, as if material progress were the sole end of his existence, and there could be nothing more to fear than present ills, to hope than present success. Those who incline to pessimism dwell on the dark side of the picture—on the symptoms of senile decay or the signs of coming storm. These I would not undervalue. The present are anxious days for the nations, at least of Europe, and most of all for ourselves. They are as dark and threatening—nay, for us more threatening—than those in the past century, while the clouds were slowly gathering for the great and prolonged storm of revolution and war. But whatever is the result to this or that nation, we may be sure of one thing—that the storm-cloud will at last roll away, and the sun come forth to shine; that the earth will once more be clothed with flowers, though it has been watered by a rain of tears and blood.

I need not pursue further this inquiry into the analogy of nature, as bearing on the alleged slowness and seeming want of purpose in the order of the world. For the individual, I admit, we can discover little ground for comfort or for hope. The most cheering message which Nature can bring to bear is that life and work are not wholly in vain. To this aspect of the case and to his position I purpose to refer in my concluding lecture. In the present one I have endeavoured to indicate that the broadening and deepening of our knowledge during the last half-century, instead of justifying any impatience and disbelief from the apparent slowness of God's work of redemption, has proved it to be in accordance with the analogies which Nature affords.

Ephemeral creatures that we are, we fancy that God leaves us to ourselves, and cares not to guide our steps, because we do not reap, so quickly as we expect, the fruit of our labours. Petulant as children in our impatience, we lay down as a condition on which our belief is to depend, that the Eternal and Omniscient God should conform to our requirements as to times and seasons and results, as though we, in our presumptuous ignorance, undertook to regulate the clock of time and the mechanism of the universe! This, at least, is the lesson taught in that great volume which ever lies open before our eyes—the only volume which some of us will condescend to read—that the growth of man to his present stage has been by almost imperceptible change, and has occupied thousands of years; the preparation of this earth for us, its masters, has been carried out, by changes yet more imperceptible, through years more by a thousandfold.

Oh the pity of it, when this tiny creature, man, this mere speck in God's vast universe, arrogates to himself the brain of Omniscience and the throne of Omnipotence! Oh the love of it, when its Maker thinks even this feeble fleeting creature worth lifting up from earth to heaven, from time to eternity!

THE PRESENT CONFLICT OF SCIENCE AND THEOLOGY (Boyle Lectures, No. VIII.).[1]

"Remember how short my time is: wherefore hast Thou made all men in vain?"—Ps. LXXXIX. 47.

If this life be all; if "to die" be "to sleep," and we must not even add, "perchance to dream"—a conclusion which, if restricted to inductions dependent on the ordinary processes of observation, we seem justified in adopting; if after death, to use the old Greek poet's words, "we sleep a long, very long, boundless, wakeless sleep;"[2]—how should we most profitably to ourselves spend this life? This is a question which, in the present day, not a few persons, who regard any belief in revelation as an illusion, seem indisposed to face. At this I do not wonder; for the question is an inconvenient one, since the answers which seem most obvious do not commend themselves to the better sense of mankind.

[1] Preached in the Chapel Royal, Whitehall, on the Seventh Sunday after Trinity, 1890.

[2] Εὕδομες εὖ μάλα μακρὸν ἀτέρμονα νήγρετον ὕπνον. Moschus, *Epitaph. Bion.*, 111.

But it must be faced, and on this subject I wish to make a few remarks in bringing these lectures to an end. Practically, as I have been endeavouring to point out, I have found myself in this difficulty—that Nature is an excellent mistress so long as everything goes well, but that she leaves me in my misery as soon as anything goes wrong. Another difficulty soon suggests itself. I suspect that by obeying her, that is, by ordering my life in strict accordance with the principles which she seems to inculcate, my actions sometimes would not harmonize with the ethics of the most highly civilized portions of the human race. Grant me a belief in a future life, which in some way will be influenced by conduct in this, and the difficulty created by this discordancy disappears. Insist that on this subject I neither know nor can know anything, except that any such expectation is most unreasonable, and we ought to face the difficulty and act accordingly. People, I think, are sometimes—it is fortunate that they are—a little inconsistent. They take their theology from Nature, and their morality from sources which, if examined, will be found dependent on revelation; and they reason as if both rested on the same foundation, and the former were to be credited with the results of the latter.

In the preceding lectures I have indicated that all

the hope, all the encouragement, which we obtain from Nature is for the race. Her care, if she has any, is for "the type," not for the "single life." Suppose the lot has fallen to me in a fair ground; suppose that I live to a good old age, in vigorous health, untroubled by anxieties, cares, accidents, sorrows; that my career runs smoothly, peacefully, happily, to its end. Then when this comes I may say contentedly, I have had my fair share of pleasure, and it is time to go to sleep. I am glad to have lived, but now submit without murmuring to the general law, and over my tomb you may write as epitaph, "I am not, and I grieve not."[1] But suppose a different lot has fallen to me. Suppose my days have been few and evil; suppose I am the victim of hereditary disease; suppose I love but to lose; suppose that, through no fault of my own—and this is often the case,—life to me, though brief, has been one monotonous record of trial and calamity: what shall I say then? This is no imaginary case. Do Siloam towers never fall on the innocent as well as on the sinners? When the Roman empire was tottering to its ruin, did the sword of Goth or lance of

---

[1] Part of the epitaph on the tomb of the late Professor W. K. Clifford, which, if I remember rightly, runs as follows:—

> "I was not, and I was conceived;
> I lived, and did a little work;
> I am not, and I grieve not."

Hun smite only the corrupt and the effete, and spare the saints? In the wild revolutionary outbreaks of France—to pass at once to modern times—were no men or women of noble lives murdered after insult, shame, and outrage, for the wrong-doing of others— wrong-doing of which they were wholly guiltless? If all ended with the fatal stroke of sword or axe, or the last pang either of agonizing disease or torture devised by man, what answer is to be given, should the victim ask this question, make this complaint: "Why has this befallen me? I have done no wrong! My birth, my life, is a monstrous injustice!" Nature can reason with the fortunate, but she has no answer for the unlucky. It is not my business to find an answer. I am glad of it; for I could not.

Let us now consider for a few moments the other difficulty which I mentioned. Would a scientific morality—as we might call one founded simply on inductive principles—agree in all points with the ideals to which the most civilized races have attained, presumably by the aid of revelation? Critics of Christianity would admit, I believe, as its friends would assert, that its moral ideal is the highest known; that man can desire no more, can aim at no more, than to live the life of the Christ. Such a life becomes intelligible if we regard the present one as forming a part of a life much more extended, as only one act in a drama ; but if not, the self-sacrifice which the Christ-like life involves cannot, as it seems to me, be reconciled with our ideas of individual justice. It may be said that society, and especially civilized society, would be impossible unless individuals were actuated by an altruistic spirit, and gave up their own good for the benefit of their fellows. Undoubtedly, the principle is true, but to what degree ? with what limitations ? Here the divergence will take place. The answer, with a rational man, will depend on the probabilities of the case. To defend myself, my family, even my state, I may endure the hardships of warfare and go so far, under very exceptional circumstances, as to sacrifice my life; counting the latter as a piece of the ill fortune to which I have already referred, because in this case I can see a direct and obvious benefit as the result. Indeed, it might even happen that, if I refused to run the risk, I might yet be killed, or only spared to find that life had become not worth the living. But in most cases, when we are considering the vague, shadowy, and extremely uncertain results which are associated with efforts to regenerate society, where we are sure of nothing but the personal inconvenience, we might with good reason decline to take more than a fair individual share of the toil.

So it will perhaps be said, " Your only motive for altruistic actions is the hope of reward." This is a possible, though an unfair, statement of my position. Reward, in the ordinary sense of the term, does not enter into the question at all. Assuming that this little troublous scene with which we are most familiar forms only a very small part of life, and that there is a God in Whom justice and love are perfect, then the statement that I shall be happier for trying to do my duty becomes a truism; it expresses an unquestionable and inevitable fact. It is, so to say, the result of a law of Nature, and to call it, or think of it, as a reward, is as much a confusion in thought and words as to say that when I am inconvenienced by cold I am rewarded by approaching a fire.

But positive as well as negative results would follow if we adopted a new basis for morality. One founded on induction from Nature would vary considerably from the law of Christ. Indeed, sometimes the two systems, if we may judge by results, seem to come into collision.

The most obvious discrepancy, as it appears to me, is difficult to discuss, but we must not on that account pass over it in silence. We may be bold to claim that in Judaism first, in Christianity afterwards, man is urged to war against the lusts of the flesh, more than in any other creed which rests on a rational basis. We may add that this teaching has been approved by the verdict of mankind—at least of that part generally admitted to be the best. "Blessed are the pure in heart: for they shall see God," is a statement which I believe few thoughtful men, however they might explain it, would desire to dispute. But would the teaching of Nature lead us to an identical result? Certainly not, if we judge by experiment, as witnessed in the case of Rome, Greece, and other heathen nations. But without pressing these instances, should we, on general principles, come to the same result? There are obvious difficulties, owing to the nature of the subject, in dealing with it in public; so I content myself with stating the conclusions which seem to me to follow, if we restrict ourselves to the teaching of Nature. They are these: that the body is likely to be more healthy when the organs duly perform their various functions; that, so far as we can see, Nature is always in favour of temperance in use rather than of total abstinence; that chastity then becomes a question, not of general obligation, but of individual temperament; and that a state of society could easily be imagined so regulated that vice, as we now call it, would be compatible with refinement and a high civilization.

But further, Christian altruism and Nature sometimes, as it seems to me, come into direct collision, by impelling us towards opposite courses of conduct. The aim of Nature, if we may so call it, the apparent tendency of her operations, is the "survival of the fittest," the development of the race to its highest standard of physical excellence (in which I include mental qualities) and to the most perfect harmony with its environment. Christian altruism has a different aim, and tends to results in some respect incompatible. It holds life to be a sacred thing, which it uses every effort to save, sometimes at no small risk and sacrifice. "Protect," it says, "the weakling infant, the helpless cripple, the consumptive, the scrofulous, the epileptic, the mentally infirm, the lunatic—in a word, all Nature's failures; keep them all alive, nurse them tenderly, give them a larger portion of time and skill and help than you bestow on the others, who, as you say, can take care of themselves." Now, what is the result of this? That you raise many of them up to become fathers and mothers, propagators and transmitters of disease; you multiply their representatives generation after generation, you deteriorate the race, and fill the world with maladies, which might have been stamped out at first by a little judicious hardness of heart. The savage who kills weakly infants, and knocks on the head the aged and infirm, is a much more logical disciple of Nature than the philosopher who, believing only in an Energy, is a subscriber to asylums and dispensaries, and busies himself in saving lives useless to the community. I do not reproach him for his inconsistency; on the contrary, I honour him for it; but that does not alter the difficulty into which I feel myself forced.

God and Nature do seem to me here to be at strife. Our efforts for moral improvement result in physical deterioration. I speak of the race rather than of individuals. I can only escape from the difficulty either by being logical and following the guidance of Nature—in which case I must expatriate myself to some place, if it can be found, which combines the morality of ancient Rome with the customs of Fiji, lest I come into collision with the law of civilized lands; or by adopting the hypothesis, as some would call it, that in this present life we can only see one chapter of a long and connected history.

Yet more. Let us assume that, by a certain course of conduct, a man becomes a benefactor to his fellows; that is to say, he gives up his life to labour for them; to helping in sorrow, sickness, and calamity; depriving himself of pleasure for their sake, and encountering noisome odours, revolting sights, possibly even personal harm. This conduct does not, of itself, conduce to his happiness. I grant, indeed, that a satisfaction is felt in the performance of what is called duty, a pleasurable emotion in the exercise of the altruistic faculties; but I am sure that, with the majority of mankind, this sensation would not outweigh the discomfort, depression, and sadness which are inevitably produced by the contact with pain and suffering.

A logically minded man, who believed that this life was all, would be forced, it seems to me, to come to this resolve: "I will take my fair share of altruistic effort, just as I am prepared to do in the case of other social duties; but it is too much to expect me to sacrifice myself for that indeterminable and uncertain end which you call 'the benefit of the race.' Indeed, our views in regard to this matter are so wanting in precision, that I am not at all sure whether these efforts are really conducive to this end, and whether it is not better to obey the law of Nature, and let the weaker go to the wall."

This, I believe, is the answer which most men would return. Depend upon it, the basis of the highest efforts of self-sacrifice is the hope, not of reward, but of immortality. Did we believe that we were day-labourers only on this earth, a paralysis, slow but sure, would creep over all our efforts to regenerate ourselves and society; our conclusion as to the best rule of life would be, "Let us eat and drink; for to-morrow we die," interpreting the maxim, not as the sensualist, but as the philosopher.

This, I believe, would be the conclusion of common sense. It will be particularly unwelcome to those who combine the exaltation of altruism with the negation of God—a combination, by the way, which, so far as it has been experimentally tested, has not worked well. The conclusion has been attacked, but the assaults upon it, and they are vehement, appear to me but so much smoke and wind—fine phrases, which will feed nobody. This epicurean conclusion, whether we like it or not, seems to me the only one which is justified by the inductive treatment of those facts which are cognizable by our bodily senses alone. It may even startle Christians; but, after all, did not St. Paul state almost the same conclusion in other words when he said, "If in this life only we have hope in Christ, we are of all men most pitiable"?

I am prepared to accept his statement; nay, I will go even further, and say that if Christianity be an illusion, it has been a doubtful gain to mankind. I am not speaking of the distorted conceptions of it which have been commonly prevalent in the world. These, at certain epochs, have made it almost a curse.

But even if the doctrine be that of Christ, I still doubt whether, so far as this life is concerned, it has added, on the whole, to our happiness. Gains undoubtedly there have been, but are not these counterbalanced by the drawbacks? His teaching has set before me an ideal which I feel to be unattainable; it has told me that the way in which I must walk is strait and narrow; that it is found only by the few, and missed by the many; that success, which alone means happiness, is rare. Hence, according to the ordinary law of probabilities, I am more likely to fail than succeed, and so, instead of being able to live my little day (the only one, as it may prove) quietly and easily, I am kept —to use a homely illustration—in a perpetual condition of strain, worry, and fever, like one who is preparing for a competitive examination. I am bidden to take up my cross daily. Yes; but I do not like it. The weight is heavy, it bruises and hurts my flesh, and no fine phrases can alter the fact of the pain. I could have lived as a philosopher—not, indeed, very happily; but if I should have hoped nothing, I should have feared nothing. This illusion has spoiled my present life, and swindled me out of my only chance of pleasure.

Denounce these conclusions, if you please, as coarse, realistic, selfish. I admit they are, when regarded from the position which I actually occupy; but if you forbid me to take this, because it rests on an illusion, then I am driven to the other, when I try to look the questions connected with my life in the face, fully and fairly, as I am accustomed to do in dealing with difficulties in science. If you forbid me to believe in a Personal God, and a possibility of immortality, then the world seems indeed to be "out of joint," and our existence to be a thing as incomplete as the design of a watch with the mainspring omitted.

Let me, then, conclude by briefly recapitulating the position which I have been led to occupy by my method of study. When I turn to the Book of Nature, its language seems to me to proclaim not only the operation of an Infinite Energy, but also of Mind and Purpose, in the main beneficent; for, though individuals ofttimes suffer sorely, yet the general result appears to be in favour of happiness, and the outcome of the struggle is the improvement of the race. I find nothing in Nature which forbids me to hope for a revelation, or compels me to deny that there can be any truths other than those which may be tested by my bodily senses. I find much in man and in his history which appears inexplicable if I regard revelation as an illusion, and his knowledge of God as a mere cloud-palace of his own imagination.

If, indeed, I do so regard it, then I am compelled to conclude that I am wearying myself in vain, that in striving to enter in at the strait gate, I have not only lost many opportunities for present enjoyment, but also have added needlessly to the anxieties of life.

So the end is this: Science does not forbid me to believe; nay, seems to go so far as to say, "Not improbable." History appears to go yet further, and to say, "Most probable." While the witness of my own heart declares that in Christ it finds the ideal which it needs, the sympathy of the human, the perfection of the Divine, nature.

If you tell me that I may not believe the story of His life because it contains incidents which are inexplicable by our present knowledge, and even contrary to our experience, I reply that to me the world is full of miracles; for it abounds with things which I cannot comprehend, and results which I should not have expected. Do you retort that this commits me to belief in every extravagant tale that wears a pietistic dress? Not at all. I claim the right of treating those as I treat startling assertions in science, by making the best use of my own judgment and knowledge, and demanding very strong evidence for what seems to them highly improbable. In so doing I am not inconsistent, for every search for truth must be conducted on the same principles.

What effect, then, will be produced on Christianity by scientific progress? In some respects, none. That which has happened has happened. If Christ lived, died, and rose from the dead, this has become part and parcel of the irrevocable past, which nothing can alter. What He said also belongs to the province of fact, and so cannot be changed; but our understanding of His teaching may be liable to modification. Christianity in the past has been well-nigh smothered under a parasitic growth of ecclesiasticism: to the root of this, science will apply the axe. It has been almost concealed beneath a superstructure of sacerdotalism: this fabric science will shatter. Vain pretensions of ignorant upstarts in priestly garb, to lord it over their better-instructed fellows; vain attempts to deter by anathemas from any honest search for truth; fruitless efforts to petrify in an elaborate system of dogma the living spirit of Christ's teaching, to stem the tide of increasing knowledge and growing thought: these science will destroy. The emancipation of Christianity from the fetters forged in ancient days is not yet wholly complete. In this great work, when the present misunderstandings are overpast, science will co-operate. Thus aided, thus enlightened,

Christianity will be able to assume a position stronger and surer than ever in the past, and those who come after us will reap the fruit of our present trials and labours in an untroubled assurance of faith, and a clearer knowledge of the Son of God than has been allotted to us in this anxious epoch of the earth's history.

THE THREEFOLD NATURE OF MAN.[1]

"May your spirit and soul and body be preserved entire, without blame, at the coming of our Lord Jesus Christ."— 1 Thess. v. 23 (R.V.).

IN reading histories, particularly those which tell us what individuals thought and said rather than what nations did, we cannot forbear occasionally wondering what would be the feelings of some of our forefathers could they return for a while to this world. How often they would find their vaticinations falsified! Sometimes the event has shown that their Utopian dreams have been baseless; that the world has only been made a very little better by the triumph of a cause to which every effort of their lives was devoted; that the seed nurtured by a martyr's blood has brought forth but a scanty fruit; but more often that predictions of evil to come have been unfulfilled; nay, not seldom that the measures which seemed to them only pregnant with calamity have proved among

[1] Preached before the University of Cambridge, in St. Mary's Church, on Sunday, March 19, 1882.

the greatest of national boons. We, in the present age, who have reached the period of middle life, cannot help wishing sometimes that this return might be permitted to us. We have lived and are living through an epoch of change and progress unequalled, perhaps, by any through which the world has passed. Whatever verdict future generations may deliver upon the nineteenth century, they cannot deny that it has been signalized by an unprecedented progress in the mechanical arts and in scientific knowledge; the powers of Nature are being pressed into our service, the secrets of Nature are being investigated with a success hitherto unexampled: what then, we cannot but long to know, will be the effect of these conquests upon the world at large? what will be the manhood of the race, whose adolescence we are witnessing? Great, whether for good or for evil, the effect must be; for, as in the organic world, physical acts upon vital, and the race, at any rate to a great extent, is the result of its environment, so must it be also in the world of thought and belief. We have lived long enough to see many landmarks, once regarded as everlasting, removed; many beliefs, once deemed sacred, abandoned; many illusions, once thought substantial, dissipated: what changes further, we cannot help asking, are in store? If we could return to life a century hence, should we find the old story of Bethlehem and of Calvary, of the first Easter morn and the first Ascension-tide, counted as among the childish things, which the adult race of men had put away, or should we find that race standing fast in a firmer though manlier faith than ours, and "the Christ That is to be" resembling yet more closely the Christ Who was in Palestine, and Who now is in the unseen world?

For myself, though I dare not say what the more immediate future may be, or whether the discipline of suffering, perplexity, and defeat may not be among the influences necessary to continue the evolution of our race, I cannot doubt of the ultimate result. Truth is great, and will prevail. But I venture to predict that religious beliefs are destined, like our social relations and scientific opinions, to considerable change, and that before long we shall see a process in the former similar in kind to that which we are witnessing in the latter. Still, as in the natural world, so in that domain which for want of a better term we call the moral and the spiritual, I believe that the ultimate result will be one of development, not of discontinuity; that there is in religious beliefs a process of evolution analogous to that which there is (though here also it may be within limits) in the organic world. So that (to take the old simile) however the superstructure of the Church may change, it will be built still on the same rock—Christ crucified and Christ risen.

I venture also to think—and it is this idea which I wish to bring more especially before you on the present occasion, though in so short a time I can only indicate one or two aspects of it—that some of the more immediate influences in what I may term the evolution of religious opinions are to come from a side commonly supposed hostile to all theology, namely, from science; and I believe that we should gain by introducing into the former more of the method (with the necessary modifications) which is habitual in the latter. Is the fact that the Eastern Magi were among the earliest to visit, and the first to bring gifts to, the newly born Christ never to be among the "things which are an allegory"? Certainly the guardians of His Church have hitherto not shown much favour to what they term "unsanctified learning," and I doubt that not a few of them would have resolutely held the door against the pilgrim strangers, notwithstanding their gold, until some satisfactory test of orthodoxy had been duly subscribed. To the elucidation of the great problem—the nature and the destiny of man—every department of study can bring its contribution.

The various sciences are capable of being helpful to Theology, not, indeed, ministering to her with hand on mouth, like servants before an imperious mistress—a view, I may remark, not seldom favoured by ecclesiastics—but as fellow-labourers in a great cause, whose provinces, indeed, are distinct, yet who nevertheless are capable of rendering much help one to another.

To prevent misconception, to which I know from experience one is always liable, I shall venture to indicate a little more fully the general nature of the changes which, as it seems to me, we may expect. The Christian creed (to use a popular term) consists partly of historical statements—a record of what are held to be facts—the doings and sayings of certain persons, especially of One, Who is, of course, Christ Jesus; partly of the interpretations which men have put upon these deeds and words. Now, the former obviously can only be altered by the removal of misstatements on points of detail. An historical narrative (subject to such correction) is either true or false. The basis of Christianity is the life and teaching of Christ, recorded in the Books of the New Testament. To regard this as legend in which there may be some substratum of fact, is for all practical purposes, as it seems to me, to reject it. We may admit the possibility of inaccuracy in isolated and unimportant details, as we are in the habit of doing in all matters of history; but after due allowance made for this, and for the idiosyncrasies of the recorders, we must either reject the Gospel story of Christ Jesus, or must accept it as we now do and as the world, I believe, will continue to accept it. But a considerable part of the creed of most Christians —the major part, I fancy, with many and the most prominent part in theology, as the term is commonly understood—consists of inferences more or less elaborately constructed from the words and deeds of the historical Christ. From the conclusions of Councils, and sometimes from the efforts of individual thinkers, has originated Christian dogma as distinguished from Christian doctrine. Now, many earnest Christians appear to regard the former as something almost Divine—nay, some are ready to say in all sincerity, of their own particular opinions, "This is the Catholic faith, which except a man believe faithfully, he cannot be saved." To deny, indeed, that in the "process of the suns" there is accretion to the sum of our knowledge, to deny that there is a development in belief as in everything connected with vitality, would be contrary to all analogy; but the important question is—How is our knowledge to be increased? Is theology to grow by processes of creation or by processes of evolution; by direct revelation through the instrumentality of

Councils of the Church or some other definite channel of inspiration (using the word in the popular, limited sense), or, as all other knowledge grows, by successive approximation—development now on this side, now on that—by the correction of over-hasty guesses and erroneous conjectures, and by the frank admission that, after certain first principles are determined, a very large field must be regarded as open to inquiry and to debate? This is what I mean by the application of scientific methods and a scientific spirit to theology. When we attempt this reformation, two principles will have to be boldly admitted; one, that the defenders of the Faith in the past (as probably ourselves in the present) have often made, even with the best intentions, most unfortunate mistakes, so as to be numbered justly among the opponents to the real progress and amelioration of the world; the other, that we cannot hope fully to grasp the mysteries of God's working, that our words and conceptions and methods of thought are all founded on the finite, and are only capable of dealing completely (if they do that) with the finite, so that we can but approximate to, not perfectly understand, those mysteries which lie beyond the veil. Hence we must be content sometimes not only to "believe where we cannot prove," but also to admit that there may be many rays of the Divine effulgence which have not yet illuminated our own particular mental horizon. Christians therefore in general, and the clergy in particular, must abandon that tone of arrogant dogmatism, and those vituperative habits which have too often characterized and, judging from the so-called religious newspapers, still too often characterize them, and must be content to admit the possibility of much divergence of opinion with regard to many points which are distinctive of Churches rather than of Christians. Perhaps a day may come when not a few so-called defenders of the faith may be regarded as among its real enemies, and charity be restored to its place as the crowning Christian virtue.

On a former occasion[1] I laid before this congregation some thoughts relating to a scientific hypothesis, concerning the genesis of plants and animals, and possibly of the human race, which is rapidly growing in favour among those most competent to form an opinion, and I endeavoured to show that, although this hypothesis would conflict with opinions commonly held, it touched no cardinal doctrine of Christianity, and left unexplained (as we should expect from the nature of the case) those mysteries which belong to the province of revelation. I purpose now to glance briefly at

---

[1] The sermons are printed in a volume entitled *Sermons on some Questions of the Day.*

what appears to me a Scripture theory of the nature of man, since it may, I think, help us in many of the difficulties which are beginning to present themselves to thoughtful persons. In so doing, I ask that we should as far as possible free ourselves from preconceived ideas in matters of interpretation. I mean that, while assuming the author of a particular Book of the New Testament to have the power of telling us something which neither we nor indeed he, under ordinary circumstances, could have found out for ourselves, we should treat his words exactly as we should do those of any other author, and try to make out (without being fettered by previous interpretations, however venerable) what meaning appears most natural to them.

The question, then, often suggests itself—What is the nature of man? Does he differ, and if so, how does he differ, from the rest of the animal kingdom? As our knowledge stands at present, a marked distinction seems to exist (notwithstanding some cases of apparent difficulty) between the inorganic and the organic world; it is much more dubious whether we can establish one between the vegetable and the animal. In both the latter, however, there is a common presence of organisms influenced by that mystery (call it force or what you will—the term will only be a cloak for ignorance) to which we give the name of life. Wherein, then, does man differ from one of the more highly organized animals? Regarded from the standpoint of science, we must, I think, admit that he differs only in degree, not in kind; for I suppose that no one now would attempt to maintain that animals possess only instinct, and not reason. As the structure and capacities of the future plant or animal are potentially present in its germ, so the intellectual powers of man may be seen nascent in members of the animal world. If, then (regarded solely from this standpoint), they are not immortal, neither is he; if he is, so are they. For myself, looking thus at the matter, I can see no other conclusion possible. If we would construct a complete psychology, we cannot obtain and we should not expect to obtain the information from science, however successful it may be in furnishing us with tests and illustrations. We cannot prove the existence of a soul by experiment, or even infer it by logical processes from observation. We must look for our information to another quarter. Revelation tells us that man is, or at any rate can be, something more than an animal, in the possession of a soul. This word, however, it is almost needless to remark, has been used with so much vagueness, that beyond the mere assertion of an immortality at any rate possible—doubtless a great point—it conveys to us little significance. But we may, I think, find in Scripture, especially in the writings of St. Paul, a far clearer statement than this word conveys—one which, carefully considered, will explain many perplexities in our complicated nature. He asserts almost explicitly, the existence in man of a tripartite nature. Body (σῶμα), life (ψυχή), and spirit (πνεῦμα). The word "soul," which I shall endeavour to avoid, is employed sometimes as equivalent to the third; sometimes (for instance, in my text) as a translation of the second; and sometimes loosely for both combined, or perhaps all three. For the first term, especially when its animal and more ignoble nature is insisted on, the word σάρξ ("flesh") is often substituted. This is the obviously perishable part; but σῶμα is possessed by the most etherealized natures. There are σώματα ἐπουράνια ("bodies celestial"). Indeed, it is impossible to conceive of personality, except as God, apart from σῶμα. If there be an *ego*—I speak as a man—there must be a limitation, a difference between the within and the without, the consciousness of which constitutes personality, and renders the former the σῶμα of that which is conscious. In this way only can I differentiate on the one hand between a mere force and life, and on the other between life, as exhibited in the world, and God. Thus, even as for life there must be a material basis, though that in itself does not constitute life, so for spirit, if it is to be individualized and exhibited in a mode in which it can be apprehended by our consciousness, there must also be a material-basis of some kind. Perhaps to some this may appear downright materialism; on second thoughts it will be seen to be a mere truism that a conscious unit is no more conceivable by us, apart from a material basis of some kind, than is light, or heat, or electricity, or any one of what we call the forces of Nature. I fully admit the possibility of the existence of spirit not so limited, but that belongs to an order of things, strictly speaking, beyond the conceptions of finite beings.

The union of life (which implies some kind of consciousness) with body makes up the animal (probably also the plant); the unity of consciousness constitutes the individual. There is a continuity of consciousness in the individual, there is also a certain continuity in the race; but in the latter—and this is true in every variation of it which may be evolved under the influence of changing environments from age to age—there is also a certain discontinuity due to the beginning of a separate consciousness for each individual. This obviously occurs whenever there are three individuals in the world where a short time before there were but two. In connection with this subject, I may add the remark, that we observe in Nature instances where an individual, a variety, or a species, apparently from failing in some way or other to comply with the conditions of its environment, becomes extinct. A branch on the tree of life, not always with premonitory withering, sometimes after exuberant efflorescence, comes to an abrupt stop; and thus so far as it is concerned, another discontinuity is introduced. In the history of life we seem to be led by insensible gradations from the simplest cell to the most highly organized animals, and I do not see that from the side of natural science we can argue for anything more. Of whatever perfection of bodily structure, of whatever perfection of reasoning powers, the animal has been or even may yet be capable, there remains, it seems to me, but one end—at last the limbs drop nerveless down, at last the busy brain is still; and what then? Dissipation of the constituent atoms; return of the localized force to the totality of the world's energy? Perhaps. Continued existence under greatly modified conditions? Hardly likely. Nothingness? Most probably.

But on the darkness of that bourne, whither sooner or later our steps must tend, revelation sheds a ray of light. It tells us of another element in our nature—a gift to man and to man alone—the spirit, the breath of God; for only by some such symbolical phrase can we appreciate what it is. This is the key-note struck in that story of its first beginning which was told to the race in its childhood, when man is said to have become a living soul; this is unfolded more clearly in another greater revelation, when it was declared to the astonished doctor in Israel " that which is born of the flesh is flesh, and that which is born of the spirit is spirit;" and this tripartite nature—this trinity, if I may be permitted the term—in man is yet more distinctly described in the psychology of St. Paul. What the spirit is we cannot attempt to define. We talk glibly of spirit, but we attach only little definite meaning to the foreign term. Perhaps to the early Christian, to whom the word was associated with the movement of the passing air—mysterious in that he knew not whence it came and whither it went, connected with all that was instinct with health and life—the term had a suggestiveness which, to us, it has almost lost. Still, though we can no more define it than life, though we can far less completely and surely indicate its phenomena, it may be very real, very true, a matter of the most assured belief. By this it is that we are made sons of God and heirs of immortality.

No passage, if I may be allowed to digress a little,

brings this out more clearly than the well-known seventh chapter in St. Paul's Epistle to the Romans. You know how difficult this is to understand; but to myself, at any rate, it has been greatly simplified by being looked at in this light. The argument seems to run thus: Man, regarded simply as an animal, a combination of body and life, a living organism, is subject naturally to a number of impulses and desires. These are not in themselves sinful; they are common to him with the rest of the animal world, and must be judged by the same standard. But the Law, embodied most completely in the Mosaic dispensation (a preparation, viewed in its effect on the race, for this new birth in Christ) made many of these sin by saying, "Thou shalt not." What is not directly or implicitly forbidden cannot be considered wrong. Sin is the transgression of the Law. The Law, however, being merely negative, had no power of quickening; it could only condemn. Its sentence was, "In thus doing as the animals, thou dost not fulfil thy destiny; thy end therefore is death like unto theirs." As the Apostle says, "I was alive without the Law once, but when the commandment came, sin became quick" (the translation "revived" appears to me liable to mislead, for the Apostle clearly does not contemplate a prior existence of sin in his own person), "and I died."

Thus even the gift of the Spirit does not deliver man from conflict. There is still the flesh, the animal nature, which ever tends one way, which, although it may be subjected to the spirit, is not changed by the spirit, and is literally, even to the end, a "body of death;" but there is also the spirit, no longer appealing only to the prohibitions of the Law, but ever pointing onwards and upwards to its Parent in heaven, ever directing the weary to the Cross of Calvary and the risen Saviour.

Revealed truth thus takes a middle ground between two erroneous extremes—an optimist pantheism and a Manichean dualism. Sin is the following of the lower instead of the higher nature, is electing to be an animal rather than a man. As the misuse of the vital powers results in a practical suicide, in the destruction of the living organism, so the neglect of the spiritual powers, the "living after the flesh," results in the death of the more perfected individual. The analogy between the natural and the spiritual life seems to hold in all respects. Each is in its beginning inexplicable, we may rightly say miraculous; each is mysterious, incapable of exact definition; each has a beginning; but who can say in either case at what moment the vital principle is individualized? In each, too, the law of the survival of the fittest operates;

and who can define the precise mode and the precise moment of death? Thus, as in all the variety of matter there seems to be an underlying unity of substance, as in all the variety of organism there seems a unity of vital force, so in all creation, from the lowest which we can behold to the highest which we can conceive, there is a unity through Him in Whom in the strictest sense of the words we, yet more fully than other creatures, "live and move and have our being."

This view of the nature of man seems to me to have an important bearing on one or two questions which are of no little importance, though perhaps their full gravity is not yet appreciated.

If scientific inquiry should result in establishing as a fact the descent of man by processes of evolution from some members of what is commonly called the animal kingdom, we may view this result with calmness, because we can claim for him the possession of a gift which they had not received. As the Christian believes that in Christ Jesus the perfect manhood was united to the Godhead in a Person Who, to the sons of men, seemed but as one of themselves, so in his own case the perfect animal has been united to the Spirit of God. If, then, we shrink from a conclusion to which a rigid theology would force us as to the fate of the myriads of human beings who lived their little day in the countless centuries of the unrecorded past, or if we find the phrase, "left to God's uncovenanted mercies," unsatisfyingly vague, we may answer, taking such a view of human nature as we have indicated, that we have no reason to suppose that they had yet been quickened by the Spirit. Or again, if another chain of reasoning drives us to conclusions as to the future of many in later times, which to us seem hard to reconcile with the idea of a God of love as revealed in the Bible, we are allowed, in that case, to ask whether this union of Spirit with living organism can never be broken, and are bidden to search the Scriptures to see what they really declare on this point. Perhaps we may find that their words, understood in their natural sense, though they most clearly declare that sin shall never go unpunished, do not necessarily establish a doctrine commonly held, and that it is doubtful whether they warrant us in interpreting *death* to mean eternal, but agonized, *life*.

On another question also such a view of Nature as I have indicated will, I think, be found helpful; namely, as to the due relation of the several members of this tripartite nature. To bring the body into subjection, to conquer the lower self, is, I think, that part of morality, whether Christian or not, which is of origin truly Divine; for I believe that a morality strictly psychic, not spiritual in origin, would allow whatever could be shown to be conducive to the health of the individual, so long as this did not conflict with the general well-being of the community. Spiritual religion declares that there are some animal impulses which must at all cost be subdued. But in so doing it does not favour the Manichean view, which some seem to have adopted, that every natural appetite is of itself sinful. The body has its rights as well as the spirit; it is the spirit's home, and I think we are justified in inferring that it is our duty to keep that home in the best repair possible. However we may admire the fixity of purpose and endurance of those men who lived the life of fakeers to conquer their lower natures, we must admit that they committed suicide, however unconscious of it they might be. They too often destroyed the better as well as the worse side of themselves; they suffered from stunted sympathies, warped affections, unbalanced judgments, and many forms of mental disturbance, to say nothing of the mischief which they did by setting before their fellow-men standards of conduct which were impracticable and erroneous. Special forms of self-denial, special acts of self-sacrifice, may be the duty of this or that individual, exactly as in the ordinary relations of life we may have to imperil and even to sacrifice it on some exceptional emergency. But the aim of the Christian should be simply to do his duty, that is, as I understand it, to accept the order of things into which he is born, and to make the very best he can of them as regards himself and as regards others.

We are living, as I have said, in times of change. No man dare predict what may await himself, still less what trials may lie before the younger among his hearers. As in each man's history there are periods of special anxiety, either from trials without or trials within, from adverse circumstances or from the rebellion of his lower nature, so is it at present with our own nation, I may say with the civilized world. Of the ultimate outcome I have no doubt; truth will triumph in the future as it has triumphed in the past; but I confess to melancholy forebodings when I see the powers of evil gathering for the conflict, and the religion, if I may so call it, of the carnal man once more attempting to replace the revelation of God, while the clergy, nay, earnest Christians in general, are too often occupied in reviving doctrines which are of dubious validity, and in claiming an authority which experience has shown that they do not possess. Still, these things may be but as the darkness that heralds the dawn; this dimness but that of the morning mists which distort and magnify every obstacle; through the breaks in these it is even now possible to discern the amber light beginning to glow in the eastern sky. Meanwhile it is our duty to labour on in patience and in trust, in the hope of doing, ere we die, some little for Christ, some little to render the world wiser and better than we found it. Our task may seem but humble, our lot in life but lowly, our contribution to the rock on which future generations shall build may seem but as the tiny cell which each single polyp adds to the great coral reef; we may find ourselves misunderstood, misrepresented, even disliked; but if we have brought some few, be they only children or humble folk, nearer to their Father in heaven; if we have shown some young men or women that the Christ Who cries, "Conquer thy lower nature and come unto Me," is worthier of love than the distorted image which his own mind or that of his earlier teachers has unwittingly fashioned; then while our epitaph may be, "I was not, and I was conceived; I lived, and did a little work," we may claim for it a brighter ending: "I am not, and yet I am; I grieve not, for I rejoice."

THE INSPIRATION OF SCRIPTURE (No. I.).[1]

"All Scripture is given by inspiration of God, and is profitable for doctrine, for reproof, for correction, for instruction in righteousness."—2 TIM. III. 16.

INSPIRATION—the inspiration of the Bible. How often is this word, this phrase, used in sermons, in arguments, in controversies! yet how perplexed many of us would be if called upon to give them a meaning! This is not without excuse, because it is always difficult to formulate satisfactorily our conceptions of things and relationships which transcend our powers. A general idea is present in our minds with sufficient distinctness to be a principle of action, yet it eludes exact definition, and refuses to be fettered by rigid statements.

But, granting the difficulty, it is unfortunate that many persons make no effort in this direction, and are content to use, in matters of the gravest moment, words, the meaning of which they do not attempt to ascertain.

[1] Preached at St. Peter's, Vere Street, Septuagesima Sunday, 1889.

At the present day it is of the utmost importance to make this effort. What inspiration means, what the inspiration of the Bible implies, has a bearing on most of the controversies of the day; and I do not hesitate to say that many a man, owing to misconceptions about these points, has been led to consider Christianity incredible, and to adopt as his creed, if we may so call it, the maxim, "We know not anything."

Many people seem to imagine that the Church of England—for with the practice or formularies of other Churches I am not concerned—has approved a particular theory of inspiration, and by it is committed to stand or to fall. This is assumed, tacitly rather than explicitly, in most of the attacks to which, at the present day, Christianity is exposed. The assailant puts to us this dilemma: "You appeal to the Bible as an inspired book. Here is a mistake in history or in science. Either deny facts or repudiate your authority." A formidable alternative. But is this really the only choice which remains to us?

Where is this definition of inspiration to be found? We search the authoritative statements of our Church, and we search them in vain. The Church of England, while assuming that there is such a thing as inspiration, while using phrases in regard to it which enable any moderately thoughtful person to obtain a general idea of her mind (if the phrase be permissible) on this point—an idea sufficient for all ordinary purposes—never commits herself to a precise and rigid definition. Look at the Sixth Article, where we should naturally expect to find it, and where we have the nearest approach. It runs thus: "Holy Scripture containeth all things necessary to salvation: so that whatsoever is not read therein, nor may be proved thereby, is not to be required of any man, that it should be believed. as an article of the Faith, or be thought requisite or necessary to salvation." The Article then enumerates the books included in the canon of Scripture, and those which are only read "for example of life and instruction of manners," but not applied "to establish any doctrine."

This cautious, guarded language stands in marked contrast with the rash statements of many would-be "defenders of the faith;" so unpalatable, indeed, is it, that by many it has been quietly ignored, by some an effort to alter it has been made. The last of these attempts, a quarter of a century since, was due to persons who, I have no hesitation in saying, ought to have known better.[1] Fortunately, it had no other result than that many men signed a document in haste of

---

[1] The reference is to the so-called Oxford Declaration, circulated for signature in the year 1864.

which I think not a few must afterwards have repented at leisure.

Let me quote a very extreme view of the inspiration of Scripture, and we shall see the dilemma in which it would place us. "The Bible is none other than the Voice of Him that sitteth upon the throne. Every book of it, every chapter of it, every verse of it, every word of it, every syllable of it (where are we to stop?), every letter of it, is the direct utterance of the Most High."[1] Obviously, the author must be speaking of an ideal Bible and an ideal translation, for that doubts exist as to the exact text in the original documents, and as to the renderings of many expressions in every text, is known to every educated person. If the author meant no more than this, then his apparently very precise statement has no substantial value, because it relates to a non-existent condition of things; probably—though I do not suppose he had yet passed from the stage of ornate rhetoric to that of careful thought—he did mean much more, and intended to intimate that no historical discovery or scientific induction can contravene any statement found in a Scripture where the text is undisputed and not of doubtful meaning.

[1] Burgon, *Inspiration and Interpretation*, serm. iii. p. 89; cf. serm. iv. pp. 93, 94.

Lay down such a canon, and what is the inevitable result? You make the authority of Scripture like that glass toy called a Rupert's drop; break off the smallest piece (and, remember, one end is very thin and brittle), and even the strong ball shivers into dust. You call upon mankind to abstain from the use of faculties which you assert God has given, and, in effect, ultimately leave them only this choice— either to submit to any guide who can persuade them of his infallibility, or to rest content with some vague form of Deism, and the hope that, if there be any future life at all, which is a very doubtful matter, they may then be comforted by some solution of the enigmas of the present one.

In what, then, may we reasonably expect that inspiration should consist? Should it anticipate the researches of the traveller, the historian, or the man of science? In the province of the discoverable, should it transfer mankind at a single step from the starting-point to the goal, and act indeed as a royal road to learning? Would there be any advantage to the race in this? Speaking for myself, I should very much like to know what was the history of the earth in the era which intervened between the first consolidation of its crust and the appearance thereon of life. To ascertain this would save me a great amount of trouble,[1] but I am not aware that it would do any very direct good to my moral and spiritual nature; and if this had been revealed to me in the past, I should have lost the education both of faculties of observation and of powers of inductive reasoning. The moral gain would have been but slight, the intellectual loss considerable. It seems, then, to me unreasonable to expect that the author of any part of Holy Writ should have been enabled to discern what future ages would discover. The most that we can expect would be that, in using the language of his day, he should be enabled to sift out that which was hurtful in its tendency, as, for example, to excise expressions or repudiate traditions favourable to idolatry or polytheism, however strongly the tide of opinion, in his era, might set towards these.

We adopt a similar position in regard to historical inaccuracies. Suppose Stephen, owing to a lapse of memory, or the author who reports his speech, did make a mistake as to the burial-place of Jacob, would that have any serious bearing on the effective value of the speaker's conviction of the nature and mission of Jesus, and of the reality of the call which enabled him

---

[1] As it happens, much of the time which the writer has spent in scientific work has been occupied by the study of the crystalline rocks, in the hope of ascertaining some information as to the circumstances under which certain of these were formed.

to face death boldly, and to perceive, beyond the things of sense, the vision of the Crucified One in triumph? If we must adopt rules of this kind in the receipt of evidence, I will undertake to leave you with very little history at all. Have you ever tried to write a description of some incident which you have witnessed, or scene which you have visited? I can speak from experience, and know how difficult it is to avoid some mistakes. Nay, I would undertake to say that if, when I had written the best account in my power, eleven other men of equal ability and care had been doing the same, our accounts would not correspond in every minute detail.

But it may be said, "You are ordinary men, not inspired." I reply that, notwithstanding our admitted fallibility and the discrepancies in our stories, you would believe the main facts to which we testified, and that you have no right, simply in obedience to some unauthorized conception of inspiration, to set up another standard for the ordinary history of Scripture. Suppose I consulted a friend of proved holiness and ripe wisdom in some case of conscience, would my opinion of the value of his advice be affected by his making a mistake in some historical allusion or illustration? We are justified, then, in attributing to historical difficulties in Scripture neither more nor less weight than we should assign to them in other ancient records.

Let us now look at the words of the text which I have chosen as being one of the few which make any direct statement on the subject of inspiration. People often quote this text as if there was no doubt as to its significance. There is really very much. The meaning of the most important word cannot be determined with absolute precision; the translation of the passage as a whole is very uncertain. As regards the former point, the phrase, "given by inspiration of God," represents one word in the original Greek. This is a compound of two words—one signifying "God," the other derived from that used for "breath" or "spirit." Thus it means that in which God may be said to breathe, that in which either His Voice, in a figurative sense, may be said to sound, or His influence becomes a motive force; it expresses, in short, by a single word, the idea conveyed in English by the phrase which obviously has a certain amount of precision and a certain kind of vagueness. But the real difficulty, as probably many of you know, is to decide upon its connection with the other words in the passage. Two renderings are possible—one, that adopted in the Authorized Version, "All Scripture is given by inspiration of God, and is profitable for doctrine;" the other, which you will find in the Revised Version, "Every Scripture inspired of God is also profitable for teaching." As a question of scholarship, it is not clear which rendering is right. Each has its difficulties, for the sentence, as it stands in the Greek, is defective, not having a verb. Each has been supported by weighty authority, but, as intimated by the change in the Revised Version, the best scholars of this age incline to the second rendering.

If this be adopted, the passage states no more than all would readily admit, and does not bring us any nearer to a definition of "inspiration."

The rendering, however, adopted in the Authorized Version is less conclusive than at first sight it seems to be. "*All Scripture*" cannot mean the Bible as we have it, unless we can show that the writer is speaking prophetically. At the date usually assigned to this Epistle, some of the most important documents now included in the New Testament did not exist, while few, if any of them, had obtained a wide circulation or had been formally authorized by the Church. The only canon then known was the Hebrew one—or the Old Testament, as we call it. Hence, even if we adopt the rendering of the Authorized Version, the passage is very far from being conclusive as to what inspiration is and to what results it leads.

We seem, then, justified in concluding that there is no real ground for the expectation—which, indeed, is sometimes formulated as an assertion—that the writers of the Scriptures and the first preachers of the Gospel should be infallible on matters of science or of history—that, in short, a revelation would be made to them in any field which was the legitimate province of human discovery.

In what, then, does their inspiration consist? We may answer this question, so far as it can be answered, by considering what we ought to expect on the supposition—and before a Christian audience I may venture to assume the truth of this—that there is a God, and that it is His will to reveal Himself to man; that the influence of spirit on matter, of the Divine on the human, is a thing not incredible and impossible, but to be anticipated as a necessary, indeed a leading, factor in the process of the education of the race.

In matters of ordinary knowledge we expect no more than we should do of other writers and witnesses, namely, that they should take reasonable care in ascertaining facts, and be thoroughly honest in recording them; we expect to find them using the language and expressing the opinions as to scientific phenomena which were current among the men of their age. We do not expect them to know the geography of lands which they had never seen; to test, by appliances yet undiscovered, the traditional history of their epoch; or to anticipate the researches in physical and natural science for thousands of years to come. But if the conceptions of their age should embody ideas distinctly false or strongly tending to produce moral deterioration, these ought to be expurgated and replaced by others which were true, and more ennobling. We expect that as time went on they would tell us more and more clearly of God, and of our place and work in the Divine economy, for we know of no process of science, no method of discovery, by means of which man, obtaining all his ideas from the concrete and the finite, can attain, of himself, to a knowledge of the unconditioned and the infinite.

By what searching can I find out God? From the phenomena of this world I may infer His existence as the simpler solution of a dilemma of difficulties, but I cannot prove it. Demonstration is impossible. What I or others have regarded as the influence of the Spirit of God upon our natures, thrilling through them like an electric current—which, hasting through the wire from an unseen and inaccessible source, is manifested at the nearer end in almost dazzling light —this influence may be no more than the vibration of the nerves, the clashing of the molecules of this bodily frame, self-begotten, self-produced,—a mere tiny storm in the tiny tea-cup of individual humanity.

If, then, there be a God, if man is to know Him and of Him, He must reveal Himself to man and through man. You who regard the Christian's creed as "not proven," you believe that there is a Great First Cause, you believe in the education of the world, in the progress of humanity. Surely, then, there is an *à priori* reasonableness in our position when we regard this education as God's work, and believe that, by processes which we can only imperfectly comprehend and by methods which we cannot precisely define, He manifests Himself through man to men, and thus is leading us onward from the corruptible to the incorruptible, from the mortal to the immortal, from the temporal to the eternal.

We believe, then, in a revelation; we believe in an inspiration, while we decline to extend it to matters with which it has no proper concern. Its function is to tell us of that which we cannot discover for ourselves—to tell us of a Father in heaven, and how we children can best draw nigh unto Him. We judge of the validity of any claim to inspiration by the evidence of the man's life, by his relationship to circumstances, by the tendency and effect of his words. We make use in his case, with the needful modifications, of the rules which we apply to all testimony and all authority, whether in history, in science, or in ethics; and in so doing we need not, I believe, be afraid to claim an inspiration for the Scriptures or to listen to the voice of God as it is breathed through the lips of men of olden time.

Some will call this a low view of inspiration. I believe that, however imperfectly expressed, it is a true view, that it will stand the test of experience, and that it harmonizes with the analogy of the Divine order in Nature. Its application to the oldest Book of the Bible is indicated in the next sermon.

THE INSPIRATION OF SCRIPTURE (No. II.).[1]

"Your fathers dwelt on the other side of the flood in old time, even Terah, the father of Abraham, and the father of Nachor: and they served other gods."—JOSH. XXIV. 2.

IN my last sermon I endeavoured to give a brief outline of the idea which the word "inspiration," as it seemed to me, should convey to our minds, and of the information which was to be expected from an inspired writer. It is my present intention to make some remarks on the application of these principles to the earlier Books of the Bible. In what sense, if any, are they inspired? Are they an infallible history of the making of the world, and the infancy of the human race? or are they a mere collection of legends, highly interesting on account of their antiquity, but with no more moral value than the folklore of any other ancient nation? In short, are they mere guesses at truth? or are they steps towards the truth, which seem to indicate a guidance higher than that of man?

These are questions of great interest and of no

[1] Preached at St. Peter's, Vere Street, Sexagesima Sunday, 1889.

small importance. Less than a quarter of a century since they were considered vital by not a few persons who would have made the authorship and authority of the Pentateuch a question on which a Church should stand or fall. Happily, they are now regarded with calmer eyes. They are still far from settled, but it is seen that the investigations of physical and historic science leave untouched the vital principles, and only modify or destroy conceptions which are of human origin or of temporary importance. We still recognize the voice and the guidance of God, though speaking in a tongue and leading by a way different from those which we had formerly supposed.

Restricting our inquiry on the present occasion to the few earliest Books of the Bible, called collectively the Pentateuch, the first question for consideration is obviously that of their date and authorship. In regard to these many different opinions are entertained, which, however, will be found to lie between two extremes—the one, which is supported by the later synagogue and by traditional Church opinion, that Moses was the composer of the entire Pentateuch, from its first letter to its last; the other, that the whole work was composed after the return from the Babylonian Captivity, though it doubtless embodies a considerable amount of earlier tradition. Those who support the latter view consider the historical value of the Pentateuch to be hardly greater than that of a collection of folklore and an epitome of opinion among the most educated and spiritually minded Jews four or five centuries before the birth of Christ. Between these extremes the truth, I believe, will be found.

To answer the question proposed above, we must glance at the history of the Hebrew canon. There can be no doubt that the Old Testament, to all intents and purposes in its present form, has existed for at least two thousand two hundred years. The date of its latest Book may be fixed, with no risk of serious error, as B.C. 420. This, then, gives one limit to our inquiry. The century succeeding the return from Captivity after the decree of Cyrus is the latest date to which any part of the Old Testament can be assigned, and before long, among the scribes of Palestine, great precautions were taken to prevent even a variation of the text.

But how much belongs to this era? Obviously certain Books, or portions of Books—such as the writings of Daniel, Ezekiel, and the later minor prophets, some of the Psalms, the conclusions of the Books of Kings and Chronicles, with the whole of the subsequent history—are later than the destruction of

Jerusalem by the army of Nebuchadnezzar. Did all the older sacred Books perish in the conflagration of the Temple, and were they reproduced from memory by those who had been their guardians? or were the records themselves preserved, and were they only revised and edited—to use a modern phrase—by Ezra and his fellow-scribes?

The former alternative seems to me very improbable; but that a certain freedom of treatment in regard to the sacred Books was permissible in the era antecedent to the completion of the canon may be safely assumed; for even those who consider themselves the most orthodox defenders of the authority of Scripture are compelled to admit the occasional interpolation of new matter into the sacred text. Indeed, one of the best and most conservative of the Old Testament critics now living in Germany [1] assures us that the equivalency of the Thorah (or the Law) and the Pentateuch is a comparatively late idea, not more ancient than the completion of the Old Testament canon.

Further, the great majority of modern scholars, including many who are earnest Christians, while they differ, as may be expected, on many points of detail, are agreed in considering the Pentateuch to be a composite work, containing at least three or four

[1] Dr. F. Delitzsch, *A New Commentary on Genesis:* Introduction.

distinct documents of different ages, and brought into its present form by the addition of fresh material from more than one hand. Sometimes the editor, as we may call him, has only quoted or pieced together older records, but sometimes he has acted as an author, though, no doubt, digesting ancient material or following established tradition. Thus in the Book Genesis three fundamental documents are recognized. In two of these the Almighty is designated by the word *Elohim*, rendered "God" in our version; in the third by the word *Javeh* (or *Jehovah*), commonly rendered "the Lord." To one of the Elohists (as they are called)—and the one now regarded as the later of the two—belongs the opening section of Genesis, as far as the end of the third verse of the second chapter; to the other Elohist belong mainly the twentieth and remaining chapters. The section between these two passages is in great part the work of the Jehovist.

Again, without entering upon further details, both Leviticus and Deuteronomy, as Books, and in a form resembling at all closely the present one, are regarded as the work of later and separate hands, though containing much very ancient material, directly or indirectly from the above sources.

To what period, then, are we to assign the various components and the completed work? Space will not permit me to give more than the barest outline. Perhaps I shall put the matter before you most clearly in a series of statements, every one of which appears to me to rest, according to the ordinary rules of scientific criticism, upon very strong foundations.

1. At the date of the Exodus the art of writing had been in existence for several centuries, both in Egypt and in Chaldea, so that there is nothing impossible in the supposition that Moses was the author of the Pentateuch, or of a part of it; for "he was learned," as we are told, "in all the wisdom of the Egyptians."

2. Many points of detail in the Pentateuchal legislation indicate an Egyptian influence, and so may be naturally assigned to an epoch while the memory of the nation's stay in that country was still very fresh.

3. The greater part of the Pentateuch is older than the Babylonian Captivity, though the last recension, including a considerable part of Leviticus, may date from immediately after that period.

4. The Book of Deuteronomy is probably next in order of age, though it incorporates a considerable amount of older material. A not improbable date for its completion would be about seven centuries before the birth of Christ.

5. To the greater part of the remainder a much

more ancient date must be assigned. There seem no valid reasons against supposing considerable portions to be documents contemporaneous with the events which they describe, though there may have been some alterations made in later recensions. Hence we need not hesitate to claim a Mosaic basis for the Pentateuch. It is no legendary tale, shaped into some kind of consistency during the later days of Judaism, but is a record, in many parts actually contemporaneous, of the nation's youth. Though it may not be possible in all cases to distinguish between original material and later accretions, the Book (speaking of it for the moment scientifically, and apart from theological questions) is an old historical work, possessing a value similar to that of the ancient records of Egypt and Chaldea.

I pass on now to the earlier chapters of Genesis, which belong, as I have said, to one or other of the oldest group of Pentateuchal documents. In order to appreciate their place in history, it will be necessary to turn away for a moment from the account of the chosen people.

When Abraham descended into the valley of the Nile, he found settled there a nation which had attained to a high state of civilization. It was even then far from young, as we count time; some of those vast monuments, which still endure, were even then comparatively ancient—as venerable, at least, as many an English cathedral. Yet more, when Abraham went forth from Ur of the Chaldees, he left behind a nation hardly less civilized—a nation whose beginnings stretch back to a past, not less, perhaps even more, remote than that of Egypt.

Let us glance for a moment at this region, the cradle of the Hebrew race, the birthplace of that Faith which is the guiding principle of our lives.

The two great rivers of Mesopotamia pass onward to the sea through a vast alluvial plain, almost as long as the British Isles, three or four hundred miles wide, and of extraordinary natural fertility. This "land of Shinar" soon became a cradle of civilization. It was occupied, perhaps six thousand years ago, by a people concerning whose aspect, language, and religion much has been discovered of late years. The Accadian nation (for so it is commonly called) was a member of the same great division of the human race as the Tartars; their religious conceptions belonged to the childhood of humanity. Each natural object was believed to have its own spirit. Their priests were sorcerers, their prayers mainly incantations. This race, in process of time, was dominated and ultimately absorbed by a branch of the great Semitic family—perhaps partly by conquest, partly by peaceful immigration. Be this as it may, the population, the language, the religion, gradually became Semitic, modified, however, by the influences of the older race. This fusion of the two nations had been accomplished long before the days of Abraham. There is reason to think that the rise of the Semitic power in the valley of the two rivers dates from several centuries before his time; indeed, the best authorities assign to Sargon, the Semite King of Accad, a date so remote as B.C. 3700.[1] The language, which was not very different from Hebrew, and the religion of this people, are now well known. In the later days of Biblical history, they figure as the Assyrians and the Chaldeans, devastators and destroyers of Israel and of Judah. Thus the Hebrew is only one tribe of the great family which in ancient days overspread so large a portion of the East. In the tenth and eleventh chapters of Genesis we find the history of their migrations in a traditional form, nations being represented as men. When we examine the records of the religion of these ancient Chaldeans, we are astonished to find therein narratives of the Creation, of a Paradise—perhaps also of the Temptation and Fall of man—of a great Flood, and

---

[1] See, for example, Professor Sayce, *Lectures on the Origin and Growth of Religion* (Hibbert Lectures, 1887), p. 21, etc.

of a subsequent Dispersion of mankind, which not only present such a strong general resemblance to, but also exhibit so many minute coincidences with, the earlier chapters of Genesis, that we cannot doubt that both have a common origin.

This may be explained by one of the following hypotheses: (1) The Jews became acquainted with and adopted the Chaldean legends during the Babylonian Captivity. This is hardly probable: for, apart from the antagonistic feeling due to circumstances, there is no doubt that, as I have already said, these parts of the Hebrew records are much older than the days of Sennacherib or Nebuchadnezzar. (2) The Chaldeans borrowed them from the Jews. But this is impossible, because the Chaldean version of the stories is much older than the age of the Exodus. Hence it seems more probable that (3) the Hebrew account was derived, at a very early period, from Chaldean sources, for the close correspondence between the two forbids us to suppose that the form of the history was any part of a revelation made to Moses. If it was derived, to what period may be assigned its transmission? Now, it is remarkable that the Hebrew story of the world's earliest days does not closely correspond with the Egyptian legends; nor does it, like the legislative part of Exodus, indicate any Egyptian influences.

After the migration of Jacob, there is no evidence that his descendants were ever in touch with the peoples of the Euphrates valley, except by way of occasional hostility, until a late period in the history of his nation. It seems, then, highly probable that these traditions were brought by the family of Abraham, when he went out from Ur of the Chaldees on his journey to Palestine.

"So," it may be said, "you reduce the first eleven chapters of Genesis to a mere collection of folklore, and deny to them the character of an inspired work?" On the contrary, I now proceed to show that, if this hypothesis be correct, they are, in the truest sense of the word, inspired. Hitherto I have referred only to correspondences in the Chaldean and Hebrew narratives; I will now briefly indicate their differences. Every one of these stories in the Chaldean version is, so to say, saturated with polytheism, for the Chaldean religion was a polytheism, and this had been further degraded by the old Accadian influences. One example will suffice. When Hâsisadra, the Chaldean Noah, goes forth from the ark, he offers a sacrifice, and to it, we are told, "the gods swarmed like flies." The Hebrew account of the early history of the world has been purged from every trace of polytheism, and it proclaims that the God of Israel is one God,

Creator and Maker of the heaven and the earth, of all that is and all that lives. By what process of mental evolution, at that era of the world's history, could a stride so gigantic have been taken? All the influences of the age were opposed to it. The stately buildings, the graven images, the polytheistic worship, the elaborate ritual of the more educated—the lingering shamanistic superstitions of the common people—all tended in an opposite direction. At such a time, under such influences, the sudden rise of a pure monotheism without a revelation is a thing, it seems to me, as incredible as Christianity without a Christ.

We claim, then, for this, the oldest part of the Book of Genesis, an inspiration in the fullest sense of the word, because it reveals to man what he has not discovered and could not discover for himself. Perhaps it may be asserted that monotheism, like polytheism, is merely a stage in the evolution of human thought. I cannot now discuss this, but will only say that I believe all the evidence which we possess points to a very different conclusion. Shamanism and polytheism seem natural to man—so natural that they often blend with Christianity and lurk under its garb. We claim an inspiration, not for the outward form, but for the moral and religious truths which the Book conveys. No man of science in the present day can regard the earlier chapters of Genesis as history in the sense in which that word is now used, but they contain important fragments of ancient tradition and relate in an allegorical form the deepest spiritual truths. The Creation of the world by the will of God is a reality, though the account in Genesis be but a poetic conception; the Fall of man is a terrible moral truth, though the tale of the apple be but an allegory; God's judgment of sin is a fact which the world will have to remember—for it is inevitable—though there was never an occasion when the waters swept away all mankind save eight persons. Some consider this view of inspiration a virtual denial of it. I retort that it *is* a flat denial of a theory long prevalent; but I ask on what authority that theory rests. And I know the answer which every honest man must give me. But I also affirm that this view is in analogy with all that we can learn of God's dealing with mankind; leading them, as we lead children, from truth to truth, declaring things as they are able to bear them, passing from allegory to fact, from symbol to idea, from the less to the more perfect truth. Thus we see that "through the ages an increasing purpose runs," and we watch the dawning of the light from its first faint eastern flush in a far-off time, till the Sun of Righteousness arose, in Whose light we walk. He it was Who said, "I have yet many things to say unto you, but ye cannot bear them now. Howbeit when He, the Spirit of Truth, is come, He will guide you into all truth."

NOTE ON PAGE 156.—The words, "perhaps also of the Temptation, etc.," were as strong as I felt justified in using when this sermon was written; but a paper, published by Mr. W. St. Chad Boscawen while this volume is passing through the press, would warrant me now in saying "almost certainly." The paper, for a copy of which I am indebted to his kindness, is entitled "The Babylonian Legend of the Serpent Tempter" (*The Babylonian and Oriental Record*, vol. iv. No. 11; 1890).

THE GROWTH OF JESUS (No. I.).[1]

"And Jesus increased in wisdom and stature, and in favour with God and man."—ST. LUKE II. 52.

WHETHER we are all eager to see ourselves as others see us may be doubted. That we like to see others with our own eyes can hardly be denied. Hence the almost universal interest felt in biographical details—an interest which may arise from motives either contemptible or commendable. The former foster a love of gossip, as it is called—that fondness for knowing all about our neighbours' business, not that we may be more able to help them, but that we may have the better chance of making depreciatory comments and indulging in self-righteous censure. This is the delight of empty brains and paltry souls, the especial fault of little or idle communities. To know how the baser sort of our fellow-creatures live cannot elevate us; to know how commonplace people live

[1] Preached at St. Peter's, Vere Street, on the Third Sunday after Epiphany, 1889.

can be of little use; but to know how the great and good have done their work in life, to hear of difficulties overcome and temptations resisted, to read of noble thoughts, of high aspirations and of unselfish deeds, may encourage us in hours of trial or provoke us to a worthy emulation. This desire springs from a right motive, and may lawfully be gratified.

In so reading a biography, I suspect that many people, if they have the habit of casting their eye over a book before studying it, glance first at the beginning and the end—at the history of the man's boyhood and of his later years. By this means they ascertain and compare the raw material, as we may call it, and the finished work—what the man received by inheritance as a kind of patrimony, and what this produced when disciplined by his own efforts and modified by his environment. Thus any one who might set himself to write a systematic biography would carefully collect and arrange every scrap of information which was to be obtained concerning the early years of his subject, and, if this was scanty, would, in effect, apologize to the reader for the inevitable deficiency.

I have dwelt a little on this topic because I wish to call your attention to the fact that the authors of the Four Gospels fail to satisfy this want, and pay no attention to an ordinary rule of biographical writers. Two of them do not say a word about the earlier days of the Lord Jesus. They begin their story with His public ministry, that is, when He was about thirty years old. St. Matthew and St. Luke give us only a few particulars. In the one Gospel these occupy rather more than thirty verses, and relate only to the days of the infancy. Between the return from Egypt and the beginning of the ministry there is a complete blank. In the other Gospel there is a little more information, occupying, perhaps, four times the space of the former. This supplies certain particulars to the history of the infancy, it tells us of a single but important incident of the boyhood, and then two verses sum up the eighteen years between the visit to the Temple at Jerusalem and the beginning of the mission work. Of these verses I have chosen one, and propose to draw your attention, in this and in the following sermon, to two points therein.

First, however, I must dwell a little longer on this artlessness or unskilfulness of the historians, because I think that in the present day it is a matter of considerable importance. Christianity is something more than a system of philosophy or of ethics. It differs from the teaching of any school of Athens, from the mysticism of Sakya-Muni, or the maxims of Confucius. It is the history of a Life, the incidents of which, to no small extent, are the doctrine and the philosophy. Far more than these other masters, Jesus taught by means of a drama in which He was the principal, almost the sole, Actor.

But, at the present day, a sort of hazy esoteric Christianity has become rather fashionable, and we are informed by its apostles that the Christ of Christendom owes more to illusion than to history. The writers, then, of the Four Gospels must be put out of court as witnesses unworthy of credit. This is often done in a very summary fashion, which may be epitomized as follows: "They must be romancing, because miracles do not happen." Well, that opens a wide question, as to the extent of the self-confident critic's knowledge (though, perhaps, here we may soon reach a limit), and as to what we mean by the word "miracle"—so wide a question that I must at present pass it by.

Assuming, then, that the occurrence of what we call miracles is not impossible, we come to this question— Are the Gospels and their authors worthy of credit? To these documents a comparatively late date has been assigned by some, who assert that they do not tell the unadorned tale of the life and death of Jesus of Palestine, but weave into it a tissue of legends which were evolved from the fervid imaginations and ardent zeal of more than one generation of excitable disciples. In respect to these allegations, we cannot, indeed, place it beyond all question that the four documents were written either by companions of the Saviour or by the men to whom they had told their story; but we can prove that, if they are not of the Apostolic age, they are but little later in date; we can prove that the narrative, in its main outlines, is that which was believed and taught by the Apostles, and that there is no valid reason (apart from the miraculous character) for doubting its genuineness.

Now, the authors of the Gospels do not write as ordinary biographers. They tell a story which is obviously incomplete. In two only of the writings do we find any sign of definite purpose. St. Luke, in the prefatory verses of his Gospel, indicates an intent of putting on record certain events which it was especially important for his friend to know, and seems to intimate that untrustworthy stories were already becoming current; and St. John obviously writes in order to bring out in stronger relief the fact that Christ was, in the fullest sense of the words, "Son of God." But, notwithstanding this, the result in every case is a series of anecdotes or reminiscences, and not a biography in any sense of the word. We can understand the gaps in the story on the assumption that the Apostles were artless and truthful writers—men of perfect honesty, but, as is said to have been the case, of little or no literary culture. But if the Gospels were in any sense the outcome of fraud or deliberate forgery, as is sometimes broadly hinted, is it probable that they would have resembled these rather disjointed and fragmentary collections of episodes? If the workman were cunning enough to frame and fashion a story so effective as that of the life of Christ, depend upon it the master-hand would have been betrayed by the more perfect finish of the work.

Thus the very defects, as I may call them, of the Gospels are a strong testimony, though indirect and unconscious, to the sincerity and truthfulness of their authors. They tell us so little about the early days of Jesus. Books, however, there are which profess to satisfy the want—books which, in a negative aspect (as I may term it), are well worth study. These are the so-called Apocryphal Gospels. Four, at least, of them relate many incidents connected with the Saviour's birth or concerning His childhood. It is difficult to fix the dates of these documents with any precision, because it is often doubtful whether the present are the original forms, and what modifications they have undergone at the hands of their editors; still, there is no doubt that many of the traditions which they have preserved are of great antiquity, and one of these Gospels, which bears the name of Thomas, is generally held to date from the latter part of the second century. The numerous anecdotes related in these books lead us to make two inferences—one, that the miracles performed by the Lord Jesus in His childhood were of a more astounding nature than those wrought during His ministry; the other, that, as He increased in stature, He did not increase in favour with man. The books tell us that He was disliked and dreaded, as One Whom it was dangerous to irritate. They represent the Child Jesus—to put the matter in plain English—as working miracles just as a clever lad might show off conjuring tricks. He does a bit of mischief, and then sets it right by working a miracle.[1] Sometimes also the miracle can be called by no other name than vindictive, as when He smites with paralysis or death a boy who had tormented, or a master who had impatiently chastised Him.[2] In short, these documents, even though they may possibly include some fragments of true tradition, are little better than a collection of idle tales, of which the chief value

---

[1] *Gospel of the Infancy*, ch. xxxvi., xxxvii., xl.

[2] *Ibid.* ch. xlvi., xlix.; *Gospel of Pseudo-Matthew*, ch. xxxviii. See also *Gospel of Thomas*.

is to bring into stronger relief the temperate self-restraint of the writers of the New Testament.

Further, if the last-named were separated by more than a full century from the lifetime of Christ, they must have known of these stories, and have put them aside, of deliberate purpose, as unworthy of credit; that is to say, they must have been, not credulous enthusiasts, but men of sufficient critical power to run counter to the dominant appetite for the marvellous, and to select from the mass of current stories such as seemed to them worthy of credit; otherwise they must have lived before these legends had obtained any currency, that is, many years before the middle of the second century. From this dilemma I do not see any escape, and commend it to the consideration of those who insist on a late date for the Gospels.

I pass on now to say a few words on one clause of my text: "Jesus increased in wisdom and stature." The latter, of course, does not require comment. It is the statement of an indisputable and self-evident fact; but the former may seem to present some difficulty. If He were God, how could He increase in wisdom? Does not this intimate that, in the writer's opinion, He was only Son of God in a more or less figurative sense? Not a few persons, from time to time, have urged almost passionately that, if any saying of our Lord's can be quoted as to an ancient historical event, the authorship of a book, or a matter of science, the question is thereby ended, and that any hesitation to accept this settlement is virtually a denial of His Divinity. It appears to me that those who thus reason lay themselves open to the charge of denying the reality of His humanity. This dilemma appears to be presented thus: The idea of God implies knowledge without limit; that of man no less necessarily involves, not only limited knowledge, but also that which is gradually gained by effort and experience. If, then, Jesus knew, as by an innate consciousness, the facts of past history or the conclusions of science for all centuries to come, the Godhead had absorbed the manhood. The assumption of human nature involves a conditioning of the Divine nature—a temporary laying aside of some of its attributes, and, in a certain sense, a diminution of its perfections. "How can this be?" you may ask. Obviously, that is one of the mysteries beyond human comprehension; but I think that the order of Nature affords analogies which may throw some light upon it. To take a very rough illustration: there may be unity of substance with great diversity of accidents, and this diversity may be due to differences in the environment. For example, carbonic anhydride under ordinary circumstances is a gas. At a certain low temperature and high pressure it is a solid. Yet its chemical composition is unaltered.

Again, without going into a long discussion concerning human nature, I may assume that, as Christians, you will admit that it is something more than a merely dynamical condition of a particular group of organisms—the thinking, feeling, conscious self is something more than the sum-total of living brain, heart, and other organs. I am conscious of myself;—that, I suppose, constitutes my personality. But there are many things relating to myself which I have forgotten; yet I am none the less myself. Still more, certain faculties may be lost permanently, if there be definite injury to the brain; or temporarily, if it be suffering from overstrain or from the consequences of physical exhaustion. But if, as the result of overwork, I should ever be in such a condition that I could not express myself clearly, or could not remember my own name or whither I was going, it would not be said that I had lost that which constituted my nature and personality (whatever it be), but only that its operation had been temporarily or permanently impeded by the defective condition of certain organisms. If, then, thought, memory, and the like, in an ordinary man, cannot be exercised unless the brain is in a certain condition of health, is it unreasonable to suppose that this organ would be incapable of discharging the functions which would be demanded of it, were it made the instrument of omniscience? In many things we require not only a mode of energy, but also a certain condition of matter to bring about a particular result. You cannot transmit electricity with a wire made of a non-conducting material. Moreover, there is such a thing as the destruction of the material owing to its very defects. Yet more, our perceptions, and thus our knowledge and powers of thought, are conditioned by our organisms. There is light which we cannot see, because its waves awaken in us no responsive thrills; there are sounds which we cannot hear, because our organs of hearing do not vibrate in reply. Is it, then, too much to assert that there are existences and knowledge to which the mind, conditioned by the limits of time and space, must be, as it were, blind and deaf? Nay, inasmuch as in certain cases the actions of the nerves and the brain in man are temporarily intensified, but this condition is ordinarily followed by exhaustion and prostration, might not the full consciousness of and communion with the Unseen be fatal to any man, perfect as his nature might be? There is a deep truth in the old belief, that no man can see God and live.

Such considerations, then, as it appears to me, indicate that we may hold that, as the Scripture itself states, our Lord Jesus Christ, during the period of His life on earth, was not omniscient. Doubtless in Him dwelt all the wisdom which would coexist with a nature free from sin and in harmonious perfection; but all matters of ordinary human learning had, I doubt not, to be acquired by Him as by any other child of man. Hence we do not dispute His Divinity when we say that, in a matter where accuracy was of no moral or spiritual importance, His knowledge may have only represented that current at the time, and so sometimes may have been defective or even erroneous.

In concluding this stage of my subject, I will only make one remark of a practical nature. The Lord Jesus, by His life, inculcated the duty of striving to advance in wisdom instead of being contented in ignorance. Obviously, it has an especial lesson for those who are young; but it must not be forgotten by any of us, for life is but one continuous discipline and schooling. The development of the body ceases at a comparatively early age, but that of the mind continues for many more years, and even when strength fails and memory is somewhat weakened there are lessons yet to be learnt of patience in trial and of spiritual insight. Many a man progresses in the highest wisdom and in heavenly knowledge until that solemn hour when "the night cometh when no man can work." There is no doubt a learning which may be useless, and a study which may be only weariness of the flesh—such were many of those subtleties of the rabbinical teachers which our Lord, during the days of His ministration, put aside almost with contempt; but the way of wisdom is the path of duty, and there is nothing sacred, nothing sanctified, in ignorance. Two Books there are whereby God reveals Himself to man, and prepares the way for the direct influence of Spirit on soul. Neither of these, as we see from the record of His life, did Jesus despise. He learnt a lesson from the lilies of the field and the birds of the air, as well as from the deeds and the sayings of olden time. What, then, God hath joined together, let not man put asunder.

THE GROWTH OF JESUS (No. II.).[1]

"And Jesus increased in wisdom and stature, and in favour with God and man."—ST. LUKE II. 52.

IN the last sermon I called your attention to the scanty information afforded by the four Evangelists concerning the early days of the Lord Jesus, and pointed out that the very defects of the record were an indirect proof of the good faith of the writers. I also made some remarks upon the first clause in the text: "Jesus increased in wisdom and stature." It is my present purpose to consider the second: "He increased in favour with God and man." This clause, like the former one, deals with two relationships, and the members exhibit a certain parallelism. Jesus increased in the sight of man, and as He grew He found favour in the eyes of man—He increased in wisdom, that is, in the sphere where only the All-seeing and All-knowing can judge aright, and in the sight of Him also He was well-pleasing.

[1] Preached at St. Peter's, Vere Street, on the Fourth Sunday after Epiphany, 1889.

"Jesus increased in favour with God and man." Let us consider the latter part first, for it offers the fewer difficulties. As I have already pointed out, the Evangelist, in this statement, contradicts the authors of the Apocryphal Gospels. The former also leads us to infer, and St. John, who passes over the earlier history of Christ in silence, virtually affirms, that He did no miracle before the beginning of His public ministry. But according to the Apocryphal Gospels, even during His infancy, His swaddling-clothes and bath-water possessed miraculous powers, and as a Child He was constantly working wonders—killing and recalling to life, changing the colour of clothes, making misfits in carpentry come right, and turning images of clay into living birds. From these authorities also we learn that He by no means increased in favour with man. We read, for example, in the *Gospel of Thomas*, "[The people] went and reproached Joseph, saying, 'It is impossible for thee to live with us in this city, but if thou wishest so to do, teach thy Child to bless and not to curse, for He is killing our children, and whatsoever He says is certainly accomplished;'" and in another place, "Joseph said unto the Lady Mary, From this time we shall not let Him go out of the house, since every one who opposes Him is struck dead.'"[1]

---

[1] *Gospel of Thomas* (second Greek form), ch. iv.

But enough of these worse than silly legends. It is not difficult to suggest a reason for the silence of the Evangelists—that it was because, from their point of view, these eighteen years afforded nothing which called for record. To outward sight, Jesus, for all this time, was a Child among children, a Youth among youths, a Man among men. That in which He differed from others would only be perceived by those who knew Him well. It might be summed up thus: that He always appeared to think, say, and do exactly what was right, and never what was wrong.

The few words which I have quoted may have been put on record to intimate the perfection of the human nature of Christ. Coming in such close connection with the return to Nazareth, they seem to indicate that the years immediately following that of the visit to the Temple were present to the writer's mind more distinctly than others, namely, those years in ordinary human life, which not only are fraught with special dangers, but also are exactly those in which the majority of youths do not increase in favour with man. Jesus, when He went up to Jerusalem, was twelve years of age, that is probably about as near manhood as an English boy a couple of years older. Now, we all know that, as a rule, boys from about fourteen or fifteen to seventeen or eighteen are not easy to manage. It is proverbially "the difficult age"—rightly called "difficult," because it does not necessarily imply that it is always the boy who is in fault. He is in a state of transition, changing rapidly both in body and in mind, and the corporeal development is commonly well ahead of the mental; indeed, the rapidity of the former sometimes disturbs the equilibrium of the latter. Such difficulty is especially likely to arise in any case where the boy possesses strong individuality of character, and is due to the very qualities which will ultimately be his distinction. It may even result from the soundness of his instincts and the honesty of his disposition, because he has not yet learnt that it is easy to make mistakes, and that caution and reticence may sometimes be counted among Christian virtues. Hence, at this epoch, as we all know, friction is apt to arise occasionally between teachers and pupils, between parent and child—with the best intentions on either side. Yet at this one also Jesus increased in favour with man.

Compared with the history of the ministerial life of Christ, this statement is suggestive, though its lessons, if common, are melancholy.

His goodness at first won Him favour with man. It is a mistake to suppose that the majority of mankind, in a fairly civilized community, have any aversion to those who are really good. It is those who are conceitedly or aggressively righteous—those in whom the existence of defects produces a want of harmony in the character, who incur dislike. To "approve the better and the worse pursue" expresses with fair accuracy the general position assumed by the multitude. So long, indeed, as goodness may be called passive rather than active—that is, when it finds expression in a narrow rather than a wide sphere, in domestic life rather than in a public career, a man is respected and liked the better for it. Even a knave, I believe, prefers to do business with a thoroughly honest man, and for that very reason will sometimes abstain from cheating him. But when a sense of duty and right compels a man to oppose a dominant current of feeling or strike a blow at some popular idol, then unpopularity must be risked, and it often cannot be avoided, though the wisdom of the serpent be combined with the harmlessness of the dove. It would be no wonder if Jesus increased in favour with men so long as He was living quietly in the home at Nazareth. Think of One Who added to the indefinable charm and attractiveness of youth, perfect unselfishness and universal benevolence; Who to the tenderness and gentleness of a woman united the best strength and vigour of a man; Who was tolerant of weakness and forgiving of injury, and yet capable of righteous indignation; who, in a word, was the embodied ideal of human nature;—such a One must have been loved, except, perhaps, by some scribe or Pharisee, whose petty notions of arbitrary proprieties he had outraged; for these men—and they did not perish with the downfall of the Temple—are most prone to call good, evil, and are most bitter against that spirit of truth and right which will not be measured with their tiny rule or fettered by their fantastic regulations.

But when Jesus began His mission work, when He came forth as a Leader of men, then He became unpopular. At first only with the legalists—with the so-called religious world. He proclaimed a reformation, and met with a reformer's fate. We know what those must expect who refuse to bow before time-honoured superstitions, and will not spare "the hoary head of inveterate abuse." This fate Jesus risked; this fate Jesus met.

His popularity with the people at large lasted longer. When faith is dying, and creeds are becoming outworn, the champions of orthodoxy are not always in high favour with the multitudes, who know too well their foibles and their faults, who have worked themselves near enough to the image, carefully though it be guarded, to see that it is not made of gold, but of clay, and that the gilding is falling off. It was not till Jesus offended the national sentiment, by proclaiming that His kingdom was not of this world, that He could find no place for a policy of revolt, and indulged no dreams of restoring an empire like to, but yet grander than, that of Solomon, that the people turned against Him, and the mob of Jerusalem joined the satellites of the Temple in the cry, "Crucify Him! Crucify Him!"

But we are also told that "Jesus increased in favour with God." This statement, like the one that "He increased in wisdom," appears to present a difficulty, and that a graver one. To increase in favour with God appears to assume an increase in goodness, and, if so, how could Jesus be truly Son of God? Moral perfection, at first sight, does not appear to admit of degree, but the phrase just quoted seems to imply a progress from imperfection towards perfection. I know well that I am dealing with relationships which are incomprehensible by man. Any expression relating to them must, on that account, be regarded from the human standpoint, and not pressed further than it will bear. But I think that, on consideration, we may perceive how it may legitimately be employed without any diminution of the true Godhead of Christ.

The key-note to the line of thought which I would suggest—for I do not propose to do more, lest I weary you—is struck in one of the earlier verses in the first Book of the Hebrew Scriptures, " Ye shall be as gods, knowing good and evil." Perhaps you will remark that the authority for the statement is the worst possible; but the devil may speak truth when he wishes to deceive. In other words, we may say that the goodness which is the result of innocence is to a considerable extent of a negative character, while that which is the result of choice is positive. To give a homely illustration, it implies no moral excellence if a man who cannot write has never committed the sin of forgery. Where there is no temptation, either because of the period of life or other circumstance, then there is no victory and no progress. By becoming Man, Jesus took upon Himself to tread a certain path, every step of which was in an onward direction. He was tempted, we are told, like as we are, though not by an innate corruption—that is to say, there was at every juncture a perfectly free and unbiassed choice between the one and the other course, which is not the case with those born after the manner of men. Sin may be defined in general terms as following the merely animal instinct when it is in conflict with a prompting which comes from a higher source. It is not, as a rule, in the act itself, but in the motive or the occasion, that the sin resides. An act—such as killing a man—is with one motive permissible or even laudable, with another a great crime. If an infant, when hungry, takes up and eats food belonging to another, this being done in innocence is not sinful; but it will be in a few years, when the laws of property are understood. Then it is known to be better to endure hunger for a while than to appease it unlawfully. Thus so soon as ever the call to resist the lower nature and to obey the higher is heard, however faintly, so soon as a person is able to see that the path before him is no longer a single one, but is parted into two ways,—then there can be the beginning of sin. To ourselves, as we all know, these opportunities for choice are afforded throughout life. At what epoch they begin, we are unable to say, but they are presented with exceptional frequency during the years when childhood is ending and the transition into manhood is taking place, because then both the faculties of the body and the circumstances of life are most rapidly changing. In some cases the choice between the right and the wrong path is not even offered until the person to a considerable extent is conscious of its nature and of personal responsibility. But with each victory won the moral nature is strengthened; so that, like a metal which has been hardened and tempered in the fire, it can be safely employed, and can be trusted in God's service. Another master has tried to lure the soul away, and it has deliberately replied, "Get thee hence, Satan!"

Thus, then, it must have been with Jesus. He passed without a blemish from the sinless Child to the sinless Man; and in so growing He progressed from mere innocency to actual and active holiness. In so doing, in so fulfilling the purpose of His mission and the ideal, hitherto unattained, of humanity, there was a perfectness at every stage; but there was also an upward progress in the stages themselves, so that we cannot refuse to say—nay, if we understand what goodness really is, we are compelled as men to say—that Jesus increased in favour with God.

Such was the development of Christ. Step by step He won His way, gathering from each age that which it afforded of good, to form the crown of perfect manhood which was to be offered on the Cross as His last and greatest gift to the race, which He did not disdain to call brothers. Of which of them, of which of us, can the same be said? Whose life is not full of vain regrets for lost opportunities and evil actions, for sins of omission and of commission? How often are we obliged to confess that our righteousness is only negative? We have not sinned, because from circumstance or constitution we have not felt the temptation. How often must we admit that, even if we cannot be charged with doing that which we ought not to have done, we have left undone that which we ought to have done!

We, indeed, forgetful of our defects, are too often tempted to echo the thanksgiving of the Pharisee, "God, I thank Thee that I am not as other men are—thieves, fraudulent, drunkards, adulterers! I have kept the commandments, and, as regards the letter of the Law, am blameless." But how far is this due to yourself, and how far to circumstances? You were shielded from temptation when young; you have never known poverty or want; you have always had little to gain and much to lose by committing a crime. If you are free from great sins, thank God's grace, not yourself. Nay, if you *have* kept the letter of the Law, are you so sure you have kept the spirit? If you have not robbed your neighbour of money, have you never by skilful misrepresentation or innuendo taken away his good name? Have you never contrived to slip before him, or even gracefully to trip him up in the race of life? Have you always cared more for truth than for your own advantage? Have you always replied, "Vade retro, Satanas!" when he has said of this world's advantages, "All these will I give thee if thou wilt do homage to me"? Nay, when you contemplate yourself, your successes and your prosperity, do you never yield to the temptation of exclaiming, with the Chaldean king, "Is not this great Babylon, that *I* have built?" Take care, O self-confident one, lest God lay thee low, even as that king who was brought to grovel among the beasts of the field. Yet, better that our Father should so deal with us than that we should go to the grave in a fool's paradise. But if we would desire a gentler awakening from vain illusions, we shall find none more effective than by keeping ever before our eyes the one Ideal of perfect manhood, Who, and Who alone, from the cradle to the Cross, so lived as to increase in wisdom and in favour with God.

THE GOSPEL OF ST. PAUL.[1]

"If in this life only we have hoped in Christ, we are of all men most pitiable."—1 COR. xv. 19 (R. V.).

SOME critics assert that St. Paul is an obscure writer; but his meaning here is plain enough. In brief emphatic phrases, clause by clause, he leads to this conclusion, "If Christ hath not been raised, your faith is vain; ye are yet in your sins." Some eighteen centuries since, in the infancy of the Christian Church, the Resurrection of Christ was a difficulty to the Greek, whether trained in the philosophy of Athens or engrossed in the commerce of Corinth, no less than His Cross was a stumbling block to the Jew. What Paul had taught as historical facts, some converts sought to explain away as misconceptions or allegories.

In this age, in this land, above all in this metropolis, where the culture of Athens combines with the luxury of Corinth, the same difficulty is felt, the same disposition exists.

[1] Preached in Westminster Abbey on the third Sunday after Trinity, 1888.

It is not surprising; scientific progress has dispelled many an error, has increased and deepened our knowledge of the order of Nature, and has thus rendered men suspicious of what they call the miraculous element in a story. It is no marvel; the Church has fostered credulity; she has now to struggle with unbelief. Reaction is the penalty of excess; this is a law of Nature, which even now Christians would do well to remember.

Thus not a few, at the present time, are offended by the Christ in Whom Paul believed. They dwell upon the improbability of the story, the fallibility of testimony, the proneness to illusion among a band of enthusiasts; they insist that neither the great fact of the love of God nor the moral beauty of Christianity are dependent upon the Pauline version of the Gospel story. Had that ended with the Cross of Calvary, the lesson of self-sacrifice, the example of boundless charity, would be not less, perhaps even more, impressive, and the love of Christ have been no less attractive had it been shown by a man to men. Love, righteousness, goodness, we are reminded, do not depend upon the attributes with which some excitable Galileans invested a leader of exceptional moral qualities. The outward form of Christianity is a mere husk, which, if it has sometimes protected, has more often concealed the spiritual kernel.

With this form of teaching St. Paul would have no compromise. He tells his disciples in so many words, "If I am deceived, and have deceived you, ours is indeed a pitiful lot." Persecuted by the heathen, excommunicate by the Jews, we have become like outcast dogs, at whom any one may cast a stone, and all for an illusion. We have chosen—poor fools that we are—a life of misery, which will be followed by an awakening, if there be one at all, of disappointment.

As I said, we are once more face to face with the old difficulties. We have to choose between a Christ purely human, and a Christ Who is much more than man. Which is to be our guide through the breakers ahead? For breakers there are. If, indeed, we live in an age when knowledge "grows from more to more," when each height attained by the toiler in science does but open a wider prospect, a grander panorama of new lands to conquer, it is also one full of dark and saddening problems—at once an age of advancement and an age of degeneration. Our land, and not our land only, is like a seething pot, wherein bubble up all that is noble and all that is base; wherein wisdom and folly, good and evil, virtue and sin, seem to leap and eddy in such bewildering confusion that no man can foretell the end, and it must be left to our grandchildren to write the verdict on this generation.

In creeds and teachers a like antithesis is found. These bid us take refuge with an infallible leader, or at least submit to directors who claim, whether officially or personally, some supernatural powers. Those declare that the order of Nature is the only fact, that the intuitions of the soul are the only safe guide. At the one extreme man claims the power of God; at the other, man almost asserts there is no God.

It is not likely that any here are prepared to go to the latter extreme, but many doubt at the present day whether Christianity, for all the centuries past, has not been resting upon an invalid foundation, and whether it be not the imperative duty of all thoughtful men in this nineteenth century "to reconceive the Christ." "To reconceive the Christ!"[1] Yes, I grant that in some sense this *is* necessary. The Christ of dogmatic anathemas, the Christ of hatred and variance, the Christ of cruel persecutions, the Christ too often of Churches,—He, it is true, was not the Christ of

---

[1] This sermon was written after reading the well-known novel *Robert Elsmere*, and the above phrase, with some others, is quoted from its pages.

Calvary. Of that Christ our conceptions, even at best, are too often grievously inadequate, warped by the imperfections of our nature and the influences of our education; but "to reconceive the Christ," so as to transform Him from the Incarnate Lord and the Risen Saviour to a mere man, though the noblest, purest, best, of the race,—is *that* the duty which is before us? We may well undertake the investigation with no light heart.

Now, as a preliminary to the few remarks which I wish to make on this topic, let me call attention to one or two points which, as it seems to me, are often left in considerable ambiguity by advocates of the new gospel.

First, there is no reasonable ground for doubting that this Epistle, with that to the Romans and one or two more, were written by St. Paul. Personally, I think others were, but as their authenticity has been disputed I will not claim them. Here, then, is a letter, dating from about twenty-seven years after the supposed Resurrection of Christ, and written by the man who did more than any other to spread the story of the Gospel. On its truth he stakes his hopes and his credit.

Again, this story in its main outlines corresponds with that which we read in the other books of the

New Testament. I am not going to assert—because that could not be placed beyond dispute—that the Four Gospels and the Acts of the Apostles are really the works of their reputed authors; but I do say that they either are documents of the Apostolic age, or relate a history which in its main outlines is identical with that believed by the Church of the first century.

Apart from collateral proofs, the latter assertion is really incontestable, if we allow that Paul wrote the Epistles which I have named, because in them the Divine nature and the Resurrection, to mention no other important incidents, are insisted on with much detail. It has been insinuated, I know, that the Christ of Christendom is largely a creature of Paul's fervid imagination, and that the testimony of James of Jerusalem, could we only recover it, would be something very different from that of Paul of Tarsus. But the latter tells us, in one of these accepted Epistles, that both preached the same Gospel.[2] This rests, no doubt, only on St. Paul's authority; but, judging from the facts of his life and the internal evidence of his writings, I should say that he was an honest and truthful man; indeed, I may even venture to assert that he would have

[1] Gal. ii. 2-10; cf. i. 8, 9.

regarded a pious fraud or a lie to serve a policy with much more scorn and loathing than some people appear to do at the present time.

But we are now sometimes informed that Paul was "so weak logically, so strong in poetry, in rhetoric, in moral passion," that he is useless as a witness. If, however, others corroborate his testimony, his personal disqualifications are of less moment, for certainly some of his fellow-workers were men of a very different temperament. But of them, I may be told, we know nothing, for it is denied that the Gospels are contemporary documents or give us a true picture of the birth of Christianity. Well, if they *are* religious romances, they belong, as I have just said, to a very early period. We are now sometimes advised to read them in a scientific spirit. I wish that men would read them in a more scientific spirit—that is, would take the trouble to compare them with some samples of the mass of literature, whether biographical or romantic, whether allegorical or devotional, which still exists and dates from the centuries immediately preceding or succeeding the birth of Christ. At what time or place will you find other men ennobled by such soul-piercing thoughts or possessed of such dramatic skill as authors of religious fiction? Victims of a strange delusion the first disciples may have been, but what gave these comparatively uneducated men the power to rise so high above the general level of the religious ideas of their time, or to fabricate a story which, if you once admit the possibility of the events, is so marvellously self-consistent and so truthful in appearance?

Further, is there any real ground for this censure so glibly passed upon St. Paul? I grant that his method of thought was influenced by his personality. He was a native of the East, not of the west; he lived in the first, not in the nineteenth, century. I grant that he was somewhat discursive, and prone, probably as a result of his education, to dwell more on verbal subtleties and coincidences than harmonizes with the modes of thought to which we are accustomed. I grant, in short, that he was a man of another age and another land than this. But, then, I ask, Was he nothing more? Certainly he was neither mob orator nor revival preacher, in the derogatory sense of these words. He was very different, with all his enthusiasm, from the founders of the Jesuit or Franciscan Orders. He has sketched out in his Epistle to the Romans a philosophy of human nature, which to many has seemed at least worthy of careful consideration. I will even venture to say that if ever that hypothesis as to the descent of man, which is now in favour with some scientific workers, should be demonstrated, we shall find in St. Paul's writings a solution of the difficulties which obviously would arise, and a means of harmonizing the results of scientific discovery with the truths of Christianity. Poet and orator Paul may have been, but he was something more. A thinker far more profound than most of his censors.

But when we have thus cleared the ground—when we have placed it beyond question that the Gospel story expresses the deliberate belief of a number of men, who certainly were not knaves and do not appear to have been fools—then we are told that we must put Paul, we must put the companions of Jesus, out of court as witnesses, because "miracles do not happen."

Perhaps, in a certain sense, they do not—of that we will presently speak; but, in the ordinary sense of the phrase, is the position thus assumed free from difficulties—I might almost say, from inconsistency? Those who occupy it accept the main outlines of the Gospel story, after eliminating or softening down the miraculous incidents, which, as they conceive, have been imported into the simple and pathetic tale by the fervid imagination and credulous superstition of the age. But, if that be so, how are we to explain the Christ, Who towers in unique pre-eminence, as all admit, high above the dull level of His epoch? What influences, what environment, were there in Judæa, or even in the then civilized world, adequate to produce a character of such moral grandeur, a soul with such spiritual insight? I grant, indeed, that there were forerunners—"morning stars" of the coming orb of light; I grant that the thoughts of these were gathered as it were into one focus by the new Teacher. But could the moral deadness of the Sadducee or the spiritual ossification of the Pharisee produce Him? Was *He* the Deliverer for whom any rank of society was looking? All these might have given birth to a leader of revolt, either religious or political; while He came not to destroy, but to fulfil—to disappoint alike zealot and patriot. If the man is the result of the joint action of hereditary tendencies and surrounding influences, how can we explain this abnormal phenomenon? Jesus Himself, as a Man of that age, was a living miracle.

Again, accepting the narrative as above stated, how shall we explain the sudden transformation of His imperfectly educated and half-hearted followers into men "full of the Spirit" and earnest in their belief? Surely the blood-stained Cross could be no emblem of hope? The knowledge that "the ashes of Jesus mingled with the dust of Palestine" would have been the despairing epitaph of a lost cause. Scorned and reviled, He had died in the sight of the multitude; claims and predictions alike falsified; and yet crushing defeat converts these timid disciples into men of high resolve and unshaken courage. There is no time, mark you, for the slow growth of a seductive myth which might at last acquire such power as to exercise a transforming influence. In a few days—that we learn from St. Paul's genuine writings—the belief in a Divine and Risen Saviour had become part of the lives of these men, so unpromising as subjects, so different in their dispositions. If there were no Resurrection, is not this a miracle, for it is inexplicable?

Further, in St. Paul's own case, the change, to say the least of it, is strange and startling. He knew the moral beauty of the doctrine of Jesus, he was aware of the new-born zeal of the Apostles while he strove to crush by persecution this revolt against ancient faiths. So sudden a conversion, on the part of a thoughtful man, as that which occurred, is at any rate difficult to explain. One explanation has been hinted; but, looking at the question as a matter of evidence, it seems to me inadmissible, for St. Paul's subsequent writings are not like those which usually emanate from men with a craze.

But, I shall be told, these and other considerations are idle. The story is incredible, because "miracles do not happen." They are simply the outcome of human credulity, always prone to indulge in the marvellous. That, we are told, is proved by the study of the history of religions; they exhibit a gradual progress from the grossest superstition and the most abject credulity to more refined and more spiritual forms. I may grant all this, without admitting more than the education of the human race and the progress of a Divine order, in which many of the critics to whom I allude believe no less fervently than myself. I admit also the tendency to see a miracle in everything unexpected, and the extreme credulity which often accompanies religious earnestness. Traces of this may possibly be found in books which we regard as part of the Canon of Scripture. But if exaggeration or possible inaccuracy in detail is to be an absolute bar to belief, I should be a victim to historic doubt after a few weeks' extensive study of the current newspapers, and end in believing nothing which I had not seen.

But let us look at the matter from another point of view. Do you believe that for yourself and others there is a possibility of an eternal life—that it is not the doom of ardent and earnest seekers after God to vanish like the morning mist from the universe of His creatures? My friend, if you have this life, how came it, whence came it? You will ask that question in vain of science. It can only tell us that for man and beast alike there seems to be but one life, and there is no reason why this should survive the dissolution of the organism. A "living soul" is no part of the order of Nature as we know it from scientific research. If you believe in the soul's existence, you must regard it apart from animal life, and obtain your assurance from other sources than those which are furnished by the laboratory. In a word, if you believe in a personal immortality you believe in a miracle.

Still, some may reply, when pressed by this argument, "Though we believe in God as Creator, Ruler, Sustainer of this world, as in very truth Father of all, we cannot believe in the Incarnation and the Resurrection, because both are contrary to the order of Nature, which is His order, and He cannot contradict Himself." I have so often dwelt upon this topic that, important though it be, I shall take leave now to dismiss it in very few words. The difficulty has no real existence, and is created by our incautious use of words. The "order of Nature" simply represents the results of observation and of inductive reasoning at this time. Our conception of it differs from that of our ancestors, and that of our posterity will differ from our own. To admit that its laws are invariable, and to claim a complete comprehension of them, are two very different things. What appears in one age to be a miracle, because it is contrary to the experience of the day, may in another prove to be in accordance with the order of Nature. In a word, our conception of a miracle is an imperfect one, due to our anthropomorphic ideas and our regarding the All-Wise and All-Perfect as if He were a man who has to alter his plans, and, as we call it, interfere with their working. There is no need that a miracle should be a departure from law—that is, from the Divine purpose and plan. The causes seem the same to us as in some everyday event, but it is a bold assumption to say that they are the same. Are not the phenomena of life miraculous when viewed restrictedly from the standpoint of physical science? The tissues of your bodies continue because you are alive, and you can give no better reason; they will quickly decompose when you are dead. Please explain this before you begin to be too confident about the order of Nature and the impossibility of so-called miracles.

Thus there is no *à priori* impossibility in the matter—the question is one of evidence; but this must be viewed in the widest sense, so as to include the position of the event in the economy of the world. Here, then, the genesis of the idea of the Risen Saviour appears to me incredible, unless He were a Being absolutely unique, Who by His birth, life, and resurrection was the crown of the revelation of God to man, the satisfaction of a longing hope, the earnest of the victory over sin and death. A Christianity without a Christ is at least as incredible as a Divine Christ.

How, then, shall we confront the days that are coming? How seek to turn their darkness into light? In the days of old, the noblest philosophy of the Gentile, the partial knowledge of the Jew, had alike been tried and found wanting. Amid the luxury of Corinth, the learning of Athens, the rottenness of Rome, Paul preaches Jesus Son of man, and Jesus Son of God—the Cross and the Resurrection. The problems are still the same, the remedy is still the same. Compassed by temptations, borne down by sorrows, man needs the help of man, but of something more than man. Looking on the grim fact of death, into the dark uncertainty of the hereafter, his faith—scorn its weakness if you will, it has to be reckoned with—his faith needs the assurance of one traveller returned from that bourne, or he will not quit the realities of the present for the chances of a future of which you can give him no certainty. Dark indeed is the path of life, with all its sad realities, unless it be illumined with the light that shone from the Easter sepulchre; sad the toil that a stern necessity has imposed upon us, unless we can hope for the rest, not of eternal sleep, but of the redeemed sons of God. Christianity, you say, has failed. No, it is not Christianity that has failed, but man's parody of it. Let Christ be preached, as by the mouth of Paul, and once more, among all the difficulties of this or of coming ages, man will with Christ die unto sin and rise unto righteousness.

THE DEMONIACS OF GADARA.[1]

"So the devils besought Him, saying, If Thou cast us out, suffer us to go away into the herd of swine."
ST. MATT. VIII. 31.

CHRISTIANS in this age of the world are often challenged to the wager of battle, as it was called in olden time.[2] We are asked to narrow the great question, whether Christianity be a substantial truth or a fond illusion, to some single issue, and stake our faith upon the result of a particular controversy. The conciseness of this process renders it very attractive to many minds, especially those of an aggressive habit. To attack is always easier than to defend. It also evokes more sympathy, for there is something attractive in the noise of breaking glass, so that most of us have a certain liking for the thrower of stones,

---

[1] Preached at St. Peter's, Vere Street, on the First Sunday in Lent, 1889.

[2] This sermon was suggested by an article from the pen of Professor Huxley, in the *Nineteenth Century*, vol. xxv. p. 169, the words of which are occasionally quoted. There were replies to it by the Bishop of Peterborough and Dr. Wace (see pp. 351, 369), and the controversy was continued.

provided, of course, that they are aimed at another person's windows.

The attack, no doubt, would be both fair and formidable if the Church of England as a body were committed to certain views of inspiration of which I have lately spoken—views undoubtedly held, once very generally, and still rather commonly, by its individual members—namely, that, allowing for certain possible textual imperfections, Scripture cannot err on a matter of science or history. But inasmuch as the Church of England, with singular wisdom, in my opinion, has abstained from committing herself to any definition of inspiration or precise statement of its province—inasmuch as I do not myself hold any such views—I venture to claim the right of the challenged person, and decline the conflict on my adversary's conditions. My belief in Christianity—I mean New Testament Christianity, not that which often passes current for it—is not grounded upon a single fact or the result of any single induction. The conclusions are reached, making due allowance for the very important differences, by processes similar to those which I have employed in my special department of science. Here I have arrived at convictions on the substantial accuracy of which I am content to rest the conduct of my work; yet I would not accept a challenge to give up my general theories, if I were defeated upon some particular issue, which had been selected by an adversary. Issues, doubtless, there are which would be fatal, and the same is true of Christianity. In regard to it, for instance, if the Resurrection of Christ be an illusion, then I have no more to say; Christianity might still be an admirable scheme of morality, and a great force tending to righteousness, but the feature would have disappeared which had hitherto distinguished it from all other religious and all other ethical systems. So I prefer to reason in a like way in all cases where direct experimental proof is not possible, and I am not going—to put the matter in plain words—to be abashed into accepting conditions on a Sunday which I should refuse without a blush on a Monday.

Quite lately we have been challenged to fight on the issue of the reality of such a thing as the so-called demoniacal possession, and particularly on the incident from the account of which my text is taken. I should like, in regard to this, to indicate, so far as may be in a few words, the reason why—though, I hope, a fairly honest man of science—I do not feel bound to become an agnostic.

Before dealing with certain details in the incident, I will notice one general objection, which was so worded as to cause me a little surprise. The destruction of the swine is thus severely censured by the critic: "Everything I know of law and justice convinces me that the wanton destruction of other people's property is a misdemeanour of evil example." As a general remark this is perfectly true, and as I do not suppose that the writer is much infected with the flabby sentimentality which is so prevalent at this epoch of our national history, I think we should very probably agree that in many cases the destruction of other people's property, so far from being a misdemeanour of evil example, was a necessity and a duty, as the only way of appealing to their feelings, and stopping them from being a curse to the world; but the insertion of the epithet "wanton" seems to me to be a quiet begging of an open question. How do we know that the destruction was wanton, *i.e.* not punitive? If the inhabitants of Gadara were Jews, the keeping of swine was an outrage on the law which at that time was their standard of right and wrong. I do not assert that they were Jews, because, as the place was east of Jordan, this is uncertain, but we must make due allowance for the fact, which at any rate is remarkable, that the incident, though so different from the ordinary procedure and teaching of the Saviour, does not appear, to any one of the narrators, to call for explanation or defence. As any act of wanton destruction was wholly unlike what we know of the Saviour's usual line of action, this application of the term "wanton," grounded on the barest outline of the facts, appears to me to indicate a frame of mind not precisely judicial.

Next in regard to the incident. The evidence in its favour at first sight appears very strong; it is related in each of the synoptic Gospels, and the marked variations in the different accounts make it more probable that these were derived from a traditional groundwork, than that they were interpolations into the original documents, as we know to be the case with one or two passages. The dates of these three Gospels in their present form cannot be fixed with precision. Two of them, however, those bearing the names of Mark and Luke, are admittedly not the work of persons who were eye-witnesses of the incidents. Matthew, indeed, was one of the chosen twelve, but in this case we cannot be sure that we possess the original document. Indeed, it would seem more probable, though there is much to be said on both sides, that this was written in Hebrew, and that the one known to us is a very ancient translation. At the same time (I say this lest I should be misunderstood in admitting thus much), I fully believe that these three Gospels are very ancient writings; that they are very probably—though this cannot be proved beyond question—the work of the authors whose names they bear; that if not, they can hardly be later than the first century of our era, and that they narrate the story of Jesus of Nazareth in all important particulars as it was told by those who were eye-witnesses of His life. But I am prepared to admit that the authors may possibly have included, here and there, an incident which formed a part of the common stock of tradition, but nevertheless might not be strictly authentic, though it might have some foundation.

Now, in regard to this incident, as soon as we begin to scrutinize it, difficulties arise. If we except the destruction of the fig tree, where also there are difficulties, and the parallelism may be disputed, this miracle is totally different from all the others which our Lord is said to have worked, but it reminds us of a type frequent in the Apocryphal Gospels and in later legends. This, however, is not all. Where did the miracle happen? St. Matthew, according to the Authorized Version, says "in the land of the *Gergesenes*," but the Revised Version reads *Gadarenes*, and one ancient manuscript *Gazarenes*. In St. Mark and St. Luke we find *Gadarenes* in the Authorized Version and *Gerasenes* in the Revised. Now, in regard to these places, the existence of a town near the lake named *Gergesa* has been asserted by commentators, but apparently on no better authority than the supposed needs of exegesis. *Gerasa* is a well-known town, but it was in Eastern Peræa, twenty miles east of the Jordan, and at a yet greater distance from the lake. Gadara can be identified with the modern Om-Keis, evidently once a flourishing town, with numerous rock-hewn tombs in the immediate neighbourhood. But this identification has its own difficulties, for the town is a considerable distance—three and a half hours' journey—from the lake shore, and the rocky slope in its neighbourhood descends to a river. Topographical difficulties, then, exist in regard to this passage which are not usually present in other parts of the Gospel history. Moreover, St. Matthew distinctly mentions *two* demoniacs, St. Mark and St. Luke only one, and there are other minor discrepancies. It is, then, evident that we are not in possession of a very accurate version of what occurred on this occasion, and thus are justified in declining to be bound by inferences founded on its details.

Still it must be frankly admitted that our difficulties do not disappear with this particular incident. In several passages of the New Testament the existence of such a condition as is described by the words "demoniacal possession" is affirmed, and the language attributed to the Saviour ascribes to Him a belief in its reality; that is to say, He employs, on more than one occasion, words which are meaningless unless addressed to a something external to the man, which, like a motive force, was the prime influence in his actions. We are, therefore, presented with this dilemma: "Either Jesus said what He is reported to have said, or He did not. In the former case, it is inevitable that His authority on matters connected with the unseen world should be roughly shaken; in the latter, the blow falls upon the authority of the synoptic Gospels. If their report on a matter of so stupendous and far-reaching import as this is untrustworthy, how can we be sure of its trustworthiness in other cases?"

As regards the latter alternative, I grant that by accepting it we do to a certain extent diminish the credit of the authors of the synoptic Gospels, but I humbly demur to the matter being regarded as one of "stupendous and far-reaching import." Reserving for a moment my full reasons for this, I content myself with remarking that, to my mind, the main outlines of the message brought by Jesus to mankind appear to me vastly more important than the correction of the diagnosis, however inaccurate, of a disease.

Let us take the former alternative, that Jesus, as man, accepted the current belief in demoniacal possession, and let us assume for the moment that in so doing He was wrong. As I pointed out on a former occasion,[1] we are told distinctly that by His Incarnation He subjected Himself to the conditions of human life, and thus to limitation, or even imperfection, of knowledge. So, it will be said, His authority in matters connected with the unseen world is roughly shaken. Doubtless, in certain matters, if that can be said to be "shaken" which we do not admit to be existent. I learn, on what appears to be good authority, that He came to bring life and immortality to light through the Gospel, and it does not appear to me, as I infer it did not appear to His special messengers, that such matters as the details of the Divine scheme of government, the nature and influences on man of beings other than human (admitting for a moment their existence), the end of the world, and the like—notwithstanding the attractions which they afford to our minds—were regarded as of primary and vital importance.

But it is affirmed the right or wrong of the idea of demoniacal possession is of such importance that a declaration on the subject could not, ought not to,

[1] See pp. 169–173.

have been withheld. This sounds to me very like the way in which children often pass judgment on the actions of their elders. They assume that they are in possession of all the facts and an equal power of dealing with them, and then have not the slightest doubt of the accuracy of their conclusions. We older folk, on the contrary, often think that their knowledge of facts is very imperfect, and that their methods of induction are very hasty.

But let us leave generalities and proceed to the particular assertion. In support of this two reasons are given. This is one: "If physical and mental disorders are caused by demons, Gregory of Tours and his contemporaries rightly considered that relics and exorcisms were more useful than doctors, and the gravest questions arise as to the legal and moral responsibilities of persons inspired by demoniacal impulses." There seems to me some confusion of thought or question-begging here. I was not previously aware that I was bound to believe that relics, or the repetition of some form of words, had any power at all of themselves. Indeed, I thought that the Church of England—whatever superstitious members of it might say—expressly repudiated any such idea. Is not this much the same as saying, "If you believe in the existence of God you are bound to worship a graven image"? The principle, in short, which it is sought to affirm—and there is nothing new in the attempt—is this: "Faith is responsible for the errors of superstition." I will alter it, so that we may see whether it will be palatable all round: "Science is responsible for the errors of charlatans." For myself, I believe the latter no more than the former.

Further, I fail to see what questions as to the legal or moral responsibility of persons thus afflicted are raised which do not already exist and have not been dealt with. They appear to me identical with those presented by the admitted existence of insanity, and I do not see in what important respect these are modified by the diagnosis of the ultimate cause of the disease. In either case a certain amount of responsibility, moral or legal, may rest upon the afflicted person, and this fact—no doubt involving great practical difficulties—appears to be already recognized both by law and by public opinion.

The other reason advanced is this—that a belief in the reality of demoniacal possession gave rise, through the special influence of Christian ecclesiastics, to the most horrible persecutions and judicial murders, and the record of a plain and simple declaration upon such an occasion as this would have rendered the long agony of mediæval humanity impossible.

I venture to question this rather confident statement. The prediction does not appear to me borne out by facts. The plainest precepts of the Gospel have been violated again and again in the name of Christ by the ministers of the Church. That Gospel which was to bring peace on earth has impelled the sword, and has been made to mankind one long agony. Read the history of the conflicts and anathemas of the early Church, of the persecutions of the mediæval and later Churches; read the tale of the Albigenses, Waldenses, Lollards, the outrages perpetrated by Romanists and Protestants, Episcopalians and Covenanters—none can show clean hands, though some are more guilty than others—perpetrated for the honour of God and for the furtherance of the Gospel of Christ, and then say if you can feel very hopeful as to the effects of a declaration adverse to the general tide of popular opinion. Men are so teachable, so ready to accept truth! Permit me to propose a test if you are the victim of this illusion. Read the New Testament without prejudice till you have fairly grasped its principles, and then devote yourself to a brief study of the so-called religious newspapers.

As regards, then, the idea of demoniacal possession. Granted that it is a belief to which human nature seems especially prone; granted that it is most intense among the most ignorant; granted that in regard to it the wildest and most absurd notions have been prevalent; granted that the general tendency of scientific study has been to attribute its phenomena to so-called physical causes,—all this, I maintain, is no proof that the idea may not have a true basis. If I admit the above facts as conclusive in a destructive sense, I must also, if I am to be consistent, abandon all belief in the existence of anything but myself, because the most absurd ideas have been from time to time entertained about everything external to myself, and then, inasmuch as I have no sure test of my own sanity, no means of ascertaining the trustworthiness of my own consciousness, I am driven to a kind of mental suicide. I see the difficulties involved in attaining to a belief in anything which cannot be demonstrated by direct experiment, but fail to see that we are placed in a much better position by practically refusing to admit the possibility of a revelation. We have, in effect, to deal with this dilemma. If we disbelieve Christianity, there is a great body of historic facts which are most difficult to explain on the theory that it is an illusion. If we accept it, we must receive as facts certain things which doubtless are incapable of experimental demonstration and contrary to general experience. This, indeed, raises a point on which I would gladly enlarge, but time does not now permit. It is this—that to say that a certain phenomenon is the result of causes wholly physical is misleading. Scientific research only discloses to us the sequence of phenomena; it in no case explains the cause. Even if you can go so far as to connect the exhibition of certain symptoms of disease with the deterioration or even the mechanical disturbance of a particular organ, you cannot say *why* it is; you have got no further than that (as most would admit) every phenomenon of life, so far as we know it, must have a physical basis. If, then, there be a God Who is the Ruler of this world— and this many who are not Christians would admit— and if man, in this world, be in a state of trial, be, so to say, at school, then it seems to me impossible to assert that there may not be creatures other than man, whether better or worse than he, who may be intermediaries in the government and discipline of the human race. When this is stated on what seems to me good authority, I do not feel justified in pronouncing it incredible on *à priori* grounds, simply because I cannot put it to experimental proof. Even in matters capable of being submitted to this test, I often cannot say *what* it is that causes the phenomena. I have never yet found any one who could really explain such a simple thing as magnetism. So, in regard to the existence of spirits of good or evil, I do not think that we can yet say more than that caution is needed, because evidently any opinion concerning them is liable to be perverted into a superstition. Further, I will add that the whole question appears to me of very secondary importance. The great duty of life, both to you and to me, is not to discuss the existence and sphere of action of angels or of demons, but to seek to follow the footsteps of Christ, and strive to come to Him, Whom truly to know is eternal life.

[P.S.—Since this sermon was written the subject has received further attention, the latest contribution being an article by Mr. Gladstone in the *Nineteenth Century* (February, 1891), which appeared while this sheet was passing through the press. The article is a learned and interesting disquisition, but seems to me to leave the main difficulties almost untouched.]

THE MIRACLES OF APOSTOLIC AND MEDIÆVAL TIMES.[1]

"There shall arise false Christs and false prophets, and shall show great signs and wonders, insomuch that, if it were possible, they shall deceive the very elect."

ST. MATT. XXIV. 24.

CHRISTIANITY is now frequently attacked, in the following way. Critics select a particular case, and present to us alternative propositions; to take one side is a virtual surrender, to take the other speedily lands us in an absurdity. It is tacitly assumed that no third course is possible.

I purpose to notice briefly one of these attacks which was published in a recent number of a well-known periodical,[2] and probably has been read by many of my hearers. The alternative which it offers to us amounts to this. Miracles are asserted to have occurred frequently in the Middle Ages. In some

[1] A sermon preached for the Christian Evidence Society, 1889.

[2] *Nineteenth Century*, March, 1889: "The Value of Witness to the Miraculous" (Professor Huxley).

instances the evidence by which they are supported is as good as can be produced in favour of those narrated in the New Testament. Will you believe both or neither? The difficulty is not a new one. No great theological learning is needed to convince us that, if the case proposed has not been already considered, it is exactly like others that have been discussed; but a seasoning of modern science acts as a stimulus to the mental palate.

Briefly, the story is this. In the earlier part of the ninth century there was living one Eginhard, secretary of Karl the Great, who, in his later years, founded a monastery of which he became abbot. He is anxious to enrich its church with some relics. A certain deacon from Rome intimates that for a consideration he can put Eginhard in possession of the relics of two saints named Marcellinus and Petrus. Eginhard sends him back to Rome in company with a trusty agent. The deacon, however, proves to be an impostor; he has promised to sell what he does not possess, so Eginhard's men steal the relics, and escape with them to Germany. As these are being conveyed to the church, where they were finally deposited, and after they have been enshrined there, numerous miracles are wrought, a few of which were witnessed by Eginhard.

Of all this he has left a record, which has come down to us in a manuscript, itself dating from the tenth century. From it we also learn, that on the journey from Rome the chest containing the relics was secretly opened, and portions were stolen by the emissary of another abbot, and that Eginhard, after discovering his loss, did not easily get back the missing treasure. The induction which we are invited to draw is as follows: In ordinary life Eginhard was a shrewd man of affairs and a sober historian, but no sooner is an appeal made to the religious (or superstitious) side of his nature than he appears to be almost as destitute of critical faculty as of moral sense. Indeed, throughout the story its chief actors seem about as conspicuous for their degraded knavery as for their fatuous credulity.

So we are expected to arrive at this conclusion: "If Eginhard's calm and objective narrative of the historical events of his time is no guarantee for the soundness of his judgment where the supernatural is concerned, the fervid rhetoric of the Apostle of the Gentiles, his absolute confidence in the inner light, and the extraordinary conceptions of the value and requirements of logical proof which he betrays in page after page of his Epistles, afford still less security."

As it happens, I have given more attention than

most people to some parts of St. Paul's writings, so may be pardoned for demurring to the censures thus glibly passed upon a highly inconvenient witness, whom it is of the utmost importance to discredit. I admit, indeed, that St. Paul thought and reasoned as a Jew and a man of the first century, not as a professor of Teutonic or Latin race, born in the nineteenth century; that, as he is speaking of things which cannot be tested by the galvanometer or the microscope, his methods of reasoning are not always in accordance with those adopted in physical science, but they seem to me at least as sound and trustworthy as many which pass muster in metaphysical works of good repute.

This, however, it may be said, is a matter of opinion, so we will pass on to consider briefly these three questions. (1) What is a miracle? (2) Have miracles ceased? (3) Is there any difference of importance between the miracles of Christ and His Apostles and those which are related by Eginhard, and similar authors?

1. Perhaps it may be well to remind you that three words are used in the Greek of the New Testament to designate the phenomena which are commonly, but vaguely, termed miraculous. These words may be rendered in English as marvels, signs, powers. The

first refers simply to the effect upon the mind of the spectators, and may indicate nothing more than superior knowledge. The miracle here consists in the inexplicability of an event, so far as the witnesses were concerned. A "sign" may be in itself quite a commonplace event, the whole significance being its occurrence at a particular juncture; the "miracle" here consisting in the coincidence. The last term—"powers"—predicates that certain persons can produce results which indicate the possession of exceptional power. Here, also, what would be called a miracle in one age would be in another an unusual and remarkable phenomenon. From this it follows that the word "miracle," so vaguely employed, has a very comprehensive sense, and includes a large number of phenomena which are only relatively miraculous, that is amazing and inexplicable. Hence the term "miracle" merely expresses an event as viewed from the standpoint either of a past age or of our present knowledge. We include in it events for which we cannot discover an adequate cause among the modes of force known to us, and which, as they are connected with the religious sentiment, are referred to the direct or indirect intervention of the Almighty. But this mode of accounting for them obviously is no more than an expression of the dominant opinion of a particular epoch; the idea of "interference with the laws of nature," though usual, is needless, and, as I think, misleading. The miracle may be the result of law as much as the fall of a stone, but of a law of infrequent operation; so that in regard to it the phrase "interference with law" is as inappropriate as it would be in the case of an electro-magnet, which, though it hinders a bar of iron from falling, so long as the current is passing, does not in any way interfere with the law of gravitation.

Further, we must not forget that these wonders, signs, and powers were not regarded by the Saviour or His immediate followers as conclusive proof of the validity of a commission or the truth of a message. The life of the prophet, the appeal of his doctrine to the conscience and moral sense of his auditors, were the only safe criteria. Christians are warned with much solemnity, and not seldom, as in the passage which I have taken for my text, that if they trusted only to the evidence of miracles, they might be deceived and led hopelessly astray. Another point also may be noticed in passing, that Christ would not work these miracles to gratify mere curiosity or stop the mouth of captious unbelief; and that the result often depended to no small extent on the mental attitude of the person relieved. Where men did not believe in Christ, there His power was not made manifest.

2. These considerations clear the way for an answer to the second question—Do miracles continue? If this question means, Have there been occurrences, since the close of the New Testament canon, which were connected with religious sentiment, and cannot be accounted for by any known physical causes?—I reply, without hesitation, Certainly. You may think that I am making a rather large admission. If so, explain such things as the effect of bad news upon the health; the influence of the will, the phenomena —endless in their variety—of hysteria and its cure. In accounting for these you must appeal to forces, as you may call them, which are not, strictly speaking, physical. Such phenomena, from one point of view, might be justly called miracles, and such miracles continue to occur. I can believe that at Lourdes, La Salette, and other like places, the imagination— the faith in a certain sense—of the sufferers in some cases has wrought their cure. But you say that is no miracle. Well, you may find a place for it in your system of the universe; you may call it an effect of the imagination, or you may devise for it a long and magniloquent name, but in so doing you neither explain it nor make it a merely physical process, as I understand the word.

I must not be supposed to assert that all the miracles related in the New Testament can be classed with the above named. There are some which in all probability will always remain as miracles to man. I simply draw attention to the relativity of the term. As knowledge grows, the sphere of the natural enlarges by gain from the outer region of the supranatural, but even these additions bring us no nearer to the ultimate causes of things, so that, turn where we will, true miracle ever confronts us.

3. There remains the question—Is there any difference of importance between the miracles recorded by Eginhard and those ascribed to the Saviour and His Apostles? Restricting ourselves to those for which Eginhard vouches—and this seems to me justifiable, owing to the circumstances of the time—one, obviously, is no miracle at all, but merely a natural phenomenon. Some spots of a red fluid appear outside the coffer containing the relics; these, on the most insufficient evidence, simply as being a red fluid, are considered to be blood. This, had it been true, would have been a mere prodigy, and without a parallel in the New Testament. The other two may be classed with the cases of "faith-healing" which I have already mentioned. You cannot explain them, you cannot ensure their occurrence like the result of an experiment, and

so far they are miraculous. But I venture to affirm that had the coffer contained the bones of any other persons, or even had it been empty, the result would have followed, provided of course the sufferer had not been aware of the change.

But there is another and yet more important difference—the character of the men and the nature of their teaching. Eginhard's emissaries steal the relics; he is a willing, nay, a joyful recipient of stolen property; others in turn rob him. As our critic remarks quite truly, we seem to be reading about the doings of a gang of horse coupers. The desire to possess a collection of relics overpowers all sense of right and wrong; the worst of all evils has happened to the men of this age, their religious feelings have led them into flagrant sin; to speak metaphorically, the devil has enshrined himself in the chapel of their souls; they are seeking to win entrance into the kingdom of heaven by deeds of evil. Is that the path which Christ and His Apostles indicated? Is that the way which leads to eternal life?

Again, what is the doctrine which these miracles supported and inculcated? It is that some scrap, whether of bone or rag, which has belonged, or is reputed to have belonged, to a holy man is a talisman of inestimable value. This doctrine might indeed be vaguely supported by an inferential interpretation of one or two incidents in the New Testament, but it is totally opposed to its direct statements. Charms, amulets, relics, and the like, are part and parcel of old-world superstitions, which Christ would have had His Church abandon, but to which its members in their weakness too soon reverted. Then the last state became even worse than the first; Christianity in its superstition more degraded than Judaism, or even than some forms of heathenism. The corruption yet lingers, its roots lie deep in human nature, and few branches of the Church, even in this nineteenth century, have wholly succeeded in purging themselves from it.

In the one case, then, we are dealing with representatives of Christianity at one of its lowest stages of degradation, a stage when men of perverted moral sense were constantly, almost greedily, expecting the miraculous to establish an immoral and thoroughly unchristian doctrine. Can that be said of the other case? The Apostles might be mistaken, they might be victims of an illusion, but can any man question their transparent honesty, their singleness of purpose, their perfect unselfishness, their noble self-devotion, their moral grandeur of life? Whither do we turn when we seek for an approved standard of right and wrong, for principles of conduct which have won the obedience of mankind, but to the pages of the New Testament, the chronicle of the lives, the words, the thoughts, of these first missionaries of the Gospel of Christ? What would Paul, what would James, what would John have said of theft and fraud and lying however pious the purpose? Their successors on such occasions have been too prone to indulge in euphemistic phrases; but they would have used plain speech and strong words. With what withering scorn would Paul have spurned these old rags and bones, these ordinances worse than Jewish, these idolized relics of weak and fallible men! It is an insult to the Apostles to make the comparison. It betrays a complete inability to comprehend their moral position; it is as if one asserted that approved character and a life of honour counted for nothing in weighing testimony, and that the existence of perjured knaves rendered worthless the evidence of men of unsullied reputation. If we adopt such canons of criticism, whither shall we be landed? Because in politics there are self-seeking knaves, is there no such thing as an honest worker for the State? Because there are quacks in medicine, are we to sneer at all physicians? Because in science there has been careless observation, hasty generalization, loose induction and irresponsible chatter, are we to abandon all trust in it, and say that some truth may be there, but that we shall never find it?

What good are we to obtain from an Agnostic position? It is that which in science we should be most reluctant to accept, for it leaves us without a working hypothesis. Is it without its difficulties? I think not. Suppose we concede that Christianity was born of a mixture of imposture and illusion, we have to account for many phenomena which are unique in the world's history, and for the part played by it in the development of mankind. The latter seems to me not less inexplicable than the idea of a Divine Founder. There are difficulties in Christianity, the Agnostic urges—certainly there are. I know them well, and the weakness, fallibility, and credulity of man. But there are difficulties also in Atheism, yet that creed—or rather no creed—seems to me logical compared with the position of the Agnostic, who halts between two opinions; who neither asserts nor denies the existence of a God; who repudiates the name of Atheist, but excludes God from the world; who cannot make up his mind whether a Creator's love and a Creator's care have been guiding men on "stepping-stones of their dead selves to higher things," or whether individual life is but a bubble on the stream, the course of nations like a river hasting to lose itself in the sands of the desert. "Behold, we know not anything," is a poor creed for this weary world. With all its difficulties, with all its alleged imperfections, Christianity is easier to believe than that God made man, with his deep capacities for loving and for suffering, and then left him to perish in the hurly-burly of life, where the individual counts for nothing, and there is no other hope than in the progress of the race. It is better, methinks, to accept the mystery of the Incarnation and the fact of the Resurrection, with their legitimate consequences, though they must ever remain to us as miracles beyond the sphere of scientific proof, and transcending our powers of thought, than to make ourselves the measure of all knowledge, and proclaim to the Creator, "Thus far shalt Thou go, and no farther."

THE RAISING OF THE WIDOW'S SON.[1]

"Jesus said, Young man, I say unto thee, Arise. And he that was dead sat up, and began to speak."

St. Luke vii. 14, 15.

If there are no other laws of Nature than those known to us, this story cannot be true. There is one bourne from which no traveller returns. Whatever weight we may be disposed to allow to the widely prevalent belief in the immortality of the soul—to use a general phrase—and in the possibility of communication between the living and the spirits of the dead, we may say that it is the result of experience, practically universal, that, so far as this world is concerned, death is the end of life. Is, then, the story true; and if so, what are its lessons?

Well, if we have made up our minds that, slightly to alter a well-known axiom, testimony may be false but a miracle cannot be true, or that "miracles do not happen," to adopt the more modern formula, it is needless

[1] Preached in St. Peter's, Vere Street, Sixteenth Sunday after Trinity, 1889.

to go further, and we must content ourselves with such spiritual consolation as we can derive from the legend. But some of us, though always sceptical as to miraculous occurrences, feel that we are surrounded by so many phenomena in our daily experience which we cannot really understand or explain, as to doubt whether this method of cutting the Gordian knot succeeds in liberating us from difficulties.

Direct proof of the truth of the alleged raising of the widow's son is impossible. All that we can do is to enquire whether it seems an accretion to the story of Christ's life, and if not, it will stand or fall with that story. Let us, then, briefly recall the circumstances of the narrative, that we may see from internal evidence whether the tale bears the marks of a fabrication. It is related by St. Luke alone. In like manner the raising of Lazarus is mentioned only by St. John, while the raising of Jairus's daughter is found in each of the synoptical Gospels. Thus the last named cannot be rejected on the ground that concurrent testimony is wanting. But if we admit the truth of one case, we abandon all *à priori* objections against the others. Really, however, it matters little whether one or all of the Evangelists mention the incident. No one can read the Gospels carefully without seeing that, according to our modern notions, they are very far from being systematic compositions; they indicate an age and habits of thought very different from our own. I think, indeed, that a better knowledge of ancient literature would sometimes make us a little distrustful of the results of measuring the documents of the first century by the canons of nineteenth-century criticism. Each of the Gospels is a biographical sketch, more or less fragmentary, so that it is as unreasonable to try them by the rules of modern historians as it would be to reject the testimony of any living writer, who publishes in a magazine some reminiscences of a friend, because he does not tell us the name of the village where that friend was born, or of the lady whom he married.

The story itself is perfectly simple, clear, and natural. Nain was a town of some size—reduced now to a paltry village among heaps of ruins—standing on the rough slopes of the hill called Little Hermon, and overlooking the upper reaches of the fertile valley of Esdraelon. The town was walled, and had gates. There is an old burial-ground near the track leading from Endor to Nain, and this route would be taken by any one coming from Capernaum.[1] The details of the incident, in their occasional minuteness and general simplicity, seem to mark the hand of

---

[1] Canon Tristram, *The Land of Israel*, ch. vi.

an eye-witness; the fact that the Saviour saw and spoke to the weeping mother before He reached the bier indicates, as has been pointed out, a perfect familiarity with the Jewish funeral rites, because she would precede the bier, the male relations and friends following it. It has also been well remarked, on this and a like miracle,[1] "The simplicity and absence of all extravagant details; the Divine calmness and majesty on the part of the Christ, so different from the manner in which legend would have coloured the scene . . . and lastly, the beauteous harmony, where all is in accord, from the first touch of compassion till when, forgetful of the bystanders, heedless of 'effect,' He gives the son back to his mother;—are not all these worthy of the event, and evidential of the truth of the narrative?" "Christ is never in haste; least of all on His errands of love. And He is never in haste, because He is always sure."

Thus we have, as it seems to me, this choice only: to believe the story a deliberate fabrication, or to believe it true, for it does not resemble a parasitic legend. I know what the latter position involves. I know that the raising of the dead cannot be demonstrated by experiment, and is contrary to the general experience of mankind. But in professing myself a

---

[1] Edersheim, *Life and Times of Jesus the Messiah*, ch. xx.

Christian I abandon a strictly scientific position, and must be prepared to accept the consequences; for this profession is inseparable from a belief in Christ's own Resurrection and in the Word made flesh; and these, though they may be made probable, cannot, I know, be proved. Once admit that Christ, in the full sense of the words, was not only Son of Man but also Son of God, and though critical laws have their place in dealing with every incident of His life, we need not trouble ourselves with any antecedent improbability of this story. In the presence of the very Source of life, the Centre of force—if the phrase be permitted—of the whole universe, what marvel if the sick became whole and the dead were made alive?

What, then, are the lessons of the incident? In glancing at these we shall perhaps see better how congruous it is with the mission of the Saviour.

Death is a painful fact—apart from sin, the most painful fact in human experience. Without revelation, as we can see from the plaintive laments of ancient poets, it was a melancholy and inevitable necessity; it might be faced with courage, it might be endured with stoicism, but all the praise and all the philosophy of man could not make it welcome, except as a release from suffering, which, after all, is really part and parcel of the same thing. With revelation, though man has found the consolation of hope and the support of faith, he has obtained an increased sense of responsibility and a deepened conviction of sin.

Suppose, however, that to those who are called away death does come as a friend; suppose that in this solemn hour the soul begins to perceive the eternal light beyond the melting mists of earth, and attains to the assurance that "to depart is far better." What is it to those who remain? Call us selfish if you will, but parting is pain, whatever blessings it may bring. Is there no blank in the home even when the daughter has gone away as a happy wife, or when the son has sailed for a distant land, though his departure be to fame and fortune which he could not have enjoyed at home? Yet these partings are but for a season; that parting is for ever in this life. Granted that "to die is gain" to the one who goes, this cannot be purchased without a loss to others. Parting is sorrow, even as pain is pain, and no poetry, no philosophy, no faith, can ever alter that fact. We may accept a sorrow as part of the discipline of life; we may receive it as from a Father's hand, in the assured conviction that it will work for our good; but welcome it cannot be so long as man is man, any more than a drug can be made pleasant to the taste by the knowledge that it will cure.

Yet more, so long as the life is strong in a man, the summons to lay it down cannot, I believe, be other than painful to himself. The preacher of old spoke truth when he said that death might be acceptable to the needy, the despairing, and the man worn out by age, but it was bitter to the prosperous and vigorous. I believe that a desire to live to the period allotted to man is not only natural but also healthy—that it is no more blameworthy than any other natural affection. It, like they, may be abused, may be perverted, but it is a part of God's order of nature, and is designed for the preservation of man and the good of humanity. Constituted as we are, it would be very seldom that a man could take up with much energy or interest a piece of work which he did not desire to finish—indeed, rather hoped he would not. So, though trust in God and the love of God enable us to say, "Thy Will be done," nature protests, and will protest whenever the summons comes, while work seems to open out before us, and the way to the grave is not yet smoothed by the gentle advance of old age. Did not Christ Himself feel this? Was not the dread hour of Gethsemane, in part at least, a protest of the human nature against the coming Cross and the abruptly closed career? What else meant that cry of agony, "Father, if it be possible, let this cup pass from Me"? But that was the prayer of the Perfect One; for it ended, "Nevertheless not as I will, but as Thou wilt."

Remembering this, we understand better the significance of those three instances in which it is on record that Christ recalled the dead to life. As has often been pointed out, the Divine power is exhibited in three stages of progress, if the phrase be permissible. On one occasion (the first, according to most authorities) the last sigh had not long been drawn; on another, life had departed at least some hours before, for the body was being taken to burial; on the third, it had lain, perhaps, four days in the tomb. But there is also a progress of another kind. On one occasion it is the child, the household darling, that is restored; on another, the young man, the sole stay of his widowed mother; on the third, the full-grown man, the blameless and beloved friend and brother. Yet all these were types of cases where nature most readily and, as we may say, most reasonably protests; for two of them certainly were young, and there is every probability that Lazarus, though we are not told his age, was still in the early prime of life.

Thus, in these three visible victories over the power of death, we see a help to faith just where its trial is sorest. Of all the perplexities and anomalies which this life offers, I think few are harder than the seemingly blindfold way in which the darts of death fly about in the world. The days of him who honours his parents are often not long, and the promised gift is not found in the right hand of wisdom. The stay of the house, the hope of the family, the unselfish worker for others, the leader in discovery, the beneficent ruler of the people, is taken away from the earth; while the idler and the selfish, the drone and the cumberer of the ground, the empty-headed fool and the designing knave, obtain the crown of an old age, though it be not venerable. How often does it seem as if death struck down the one in a household, in a village, in a town, in a country, who was most sorely needed, and spared a thousand whom nobody would have regretted? Are these the ways, poor and heart-broken human nature is tempted to cry—are these the ways of a heavenly Father? Does He care for us? May not those, after all, be right who said that the gods lay beside their nectar careless of this world's trials, and even found

> "A music centred in a doleful song
> Steaming up, a lamentation and an ancient tale of wrong"? [1]

The faith is strong that has never felt this temptation. Why, we ask, is the old epitaph, "But shown to earth,"

---

[1] Tennyson, *The Lotus Eaters*.

so often true? Why is there so often a survival of the unfittest—at least, for all the nobler ends of man—rather than of the fittest?

We ask the question, and of ourselves we can give it no answer. We may reply that, as a rule, vice shortens and temperance prolongs life, but the exceptional cases are numerous, and every one knows that the issue of life and death is not in his own hands, for no armour that man can make is without a joint where the dart of death can penetrate. We can say no more than that this is a dark mystery, and vaguely hope that it will some day be cleared up. In the light of revelation the mystery still remains, but it becomes less dark. One doubt, at any rate, disappears. The trouble comes by the Will of God. Jesus was, in very truth, the Resurrection and the Life. It needed but a word from Him to bring back the spirit when it had fled from the body. Therefore He permits the trial; He, in a sense, lays the burden upon us. Trial it is, burden it is; that He knows, that He acknowledged by His tears at the tomb of Lazarus, by His intervention in these three cases, each of which would have been numbered by us among the more perplexing and peculiar hardships. Is the little one gone, just when childhood's charm is sweetest? Is the young man gone, just when we miss him most?

Is the worker called, just when our need is sorest? Jesus could have called them back. To Him there is no limitation of place. He is as near to us now as He was to that mourning procession at the gate of Nain. Though passed away from this earth, He has not lost the power of sympathy with human infirmity and human sorrow; and if He let these trials visit us, if He let our bodies be racked with pain or our hearts be wrung with sorrow, we may be sure that this is no mere chance, no accident from the rolling wheels of some vast insensate machine, no apathy on His part, but the correction of a loving Hand, which will lead us, though by a way which is dark, and a path which is hard, to a land better than earth, beautiful as it often is; to a life better than this, great as its pleasures and grand as its opportunities may be. Earth is fair, but there may be worlds fairer yet; work is sweet, but there may be labour yet more welcome, in which weariness never comes and failure is never known.

Thus, though sorrow and pain cannot be dismissed from our lives, though they remain as bitter facts in the economy of this world, which no faith and no trust can make other than they are, still the life of Jesus has enabled us to bear them with a new spirit, because He has shown the world more clearly than it had ever known before that all does not end with the parting breath, and that notwithstanding man's weaknesses, follies, and infirmities, He loves those for whom He was willing to die with a love which passeth knowledge. We, then, though we do not cease to suffer or to sorrow, no longer do this as those who have no hope. Believing where we cannot prove, trusting where we cannot understand, we can cast all our care upon Him, knowing that He careth for us; and though we are often forced to cry with Him, "Let this cup pass from me," we, too, learn at last to add, "Nevertheless not my will, but Thine, be done."

PATIENCE IN WORK.[1]

"Be patient therefore, brethren, unto the coming of the Lord. Behold, the husbandman waiteth for the precious fruit of the earth, and hath long patience for it, until he receive the early and latter rain."—ST. JAMES v. 7.

THE key-note sounded in these words is one which should be dominant in every great undertaking, most of all in that to which you dedicate yourselves to-day. It would be easy to find one which, like the sound of a trumpet, seemed at first sight better fitted to stir the heart and awaken enthusiasm, but none which in my opinion is so much needed, especially at the present time.

The Apostle bids his hearers to be content to sow, and to wait till the appointed season before they expect to reap the fruits. The husbandman in Palestine sows the seed in the late autumn; then come the November rains, when he must perforce leave it to lie in the ground. Again, at the end of the

[1] Preached at the Ordination in Manchester Cathedral on the Fourth Sunday in Advent, 1887.

winter, there is another rainy period, preventing field-work; then, in the month of May, some half a year after the sowing, he puts the sickle into the corn. During this period he has had to work, to wait, and even to watch, knowing always that he could not accelerate the ripening by a single day. Laws were in operation over which he had no control. The most that he could do was to give them free play by removing impediments and by counteracting obstacles.

The Apostle refers us to a law of nature, that is, to a law of God. As was the wont of his Master, he grounds his teaching upon the order of nature. To this we are constantly referred for lessons in the earlier days of Christianity; for the divorce of what God hath joined together is the outcome of a later age, and a less healthy faith. The more carefully we consider it, the more shall we see that nature has analogies with grace, and that diverse as they may seem in their modes of manifestation, there is an underlying unity in the spiritual, like that in the material forces.

What laws, then, do we see working in nature? Two especially—the law of continuity and the law of development. The law of continuity: that is to say, that every event at any time is the outcome of a long series of antecedent causes; the law of development: that from the germ comes the seedling, from the mature plant the flower, and from the flower at last the fruit.

Students of science for years past have been engaged in deciphering the picture-writing of the book of Nature. The result of their labours has been to carry us back into a far-distant past. We are enabled to behold the surface of this globe as it solidifies in cooling, to watch the gathering of seas in its depressions, until after many years it becomes habitable by living creatures. These at first are simple in organization, less specialized in their functions than those of succeeding ages. As time proceeds we note the appearance of new types of plants and animals, higher in the scale of being—" the old order changing, yielding place to new," until at last man enters upon the scene, the first being of whom it could be said that he was made in the image of God. In the uniformity of this order there are indeed minor catastrophic changes; birth and death also are discontinuities in the individual life, but with these exceptions continuity and development are the laws which we formulate by induction from our observation of the order of nature.

The testimony of history leads to the same

conclusion, when its facts receive inductive treatment, and this, as the only scientific method, is alone likely to produce any really useful results. Those unnumbered centuries which fade away into the distant past, the fragmental records of which are being slowly recovered and pieced together by students—those centuries exhibit one long preparation for the coming of Christ, and the establishment of a spiritual kingdom. In those distant ages we can now see men, as it were, feeling in the darkness after God, gradually laying aside the imperfect conceptions and puerile superstitions of the childhood of a race. We can watch the growth of a deeper sense of human unworthiness, of a clearer apprehension of the Divine perfection, of a purer morality, of a more assured faith, and of an eternal hope. So that in the Gospel all that is best and noblest in the teaching of sage and prophet alike is embodied, and we recognize thankfully and hopefully the work of the preparation of man in the long period of the dawn which heralded the rising of the Sun of Righteousness.

But even then the process of development was not ended. In the order of nature the actual rising of the sun is an epoch of rapid passage from shadow into light; yet as the hours advance towards noon, that light increases in brilliancy and intensity. So has it been in the centuries which have elapsed since the first great Advent. True, that after the analogy of the natural day there have been clouds which have obscured the light; true, that the darkest and most misleading in their effects, like the fogs of a great city, have been mainly of man's own raising; true, that the tendency towards deterioration or hurtful exaggeration, bringing as its penalty the "Nemesis of disproportion," has produced so much sorrow, suffering, and superstition, that we are sometimes tempted to think that no sacrifice would be too great could we recover the clear light and the fresh coolness of those early hours. Yet, although these evil tendencies have done their worst, although too often the spiritual guides of our race have led their flocks back into air infected by pagan idolatries, instead of upwards on the slopes of the Mount of God; yet, notwithstanding, that race as a whole has attained a higher standard of moral consciousness, and to us a better, because a less imperfect, knowledge of God is possible than it was to the Christian of the first century.

We often hear the lament that this is a sceptical age. We are told that men no longer listen to the voice of the Church. Certainly when her representatives talk nonsense, men tell them so in very plain terms. If that were all, I for one should make no complaint. The only difference I can recognize between ordinary nonsense and religious nonsense is that the latter is more mischievous than the former, and so should have the prompter treatment from the besom of destruction. But undoubtedly, apart from this prevalence to outspoken criticism, in itself a healthy feature, and salutary, if unpleasant, to those exposed to it—the present is an anxious time. He would be a bold man who would venture to predict what will be the state of England in the beginning of the coming century. A cloud has been rising and gathering for some years, and now darkens the sky; a cloud, where the destructive electricity of rapine and murder and the vilest tyranny is concealed in the vapours of high-sounding phrases of universal benevolence and virtue. But if this cloud, as has happened before, and I pray may happen again, be dissipated by the unquenchable light of Christ's Gospel, then I predict there will be for the coming age a stronger faith: for it will be founded on a clearer knowledge, it will be the faith of the man as compared with the faith of the youth.

Into the arena of contest, at this important crisis of our national history, you are this day about to descend. Let me, then, for a few moments, call attention to a very great danger and a very great temptation to which you will all be exposed. The danger and the temptation are the outcome of an infection in the spirit of the age, and it is one suggested by the text which I have chosen, and the remarks which I have been making.

In one word, a fault, perhaps the fault, of the age is impatience. Whatever is done in the present day, we must have " results," as we call them. Well, I am as opposed as any man can be to a waste either of time or of money, but I consider worthless results, bad results, as in some ways worse than no results at all. A house built in a hurry is pretty sure to double its cost in endless repairs before many years are over, and is very apt to tumble down on the heads of its occupants. So is it with all the work inspired by an impatient spirit. God has set in the world His laws of continuity and development. We, in our conceit, imagine that we can overrule those laws. You may as reasonably flatter yourselves that you can gather summer fruits in this country for Christmas Day, or alter the position of the earth's axis of rotation.

By this feverish impatience the whole community is more or less infected, but it works thus on Christian societies. Our own branch of the Church, in common with other religious communities, has become of late years keenly conscious of past shortcomings, and is animated by an earnest zeal to win to Christ the multitudes in this and other lands who are now living literally without God in the world. Against such a zeal I would be the last to protest, but must nevertheless impress upon you that if divorced from discretion it may do much harm, possibly so much as to overcome the good. "We must attract the people," is the constant cry of ministers of the Gospel at the present day. Certainly, but how? Are any means justifiable? No one in his senses would answer that question in the affirmative. So it is tacitly admitted that there are means which it is neither wise nor right to employ, and we must regard them as well as the end. Now, with a great number of earnest workers at the present day the means most in favour are founded on an appeal only to the emotions. This appeal takes very diverse, sometimes antagonistic, forms. By some men the results and consequences of sin are depicted in such glowing terms that the auditors are lashed into an hysteric condition, which, transitory though it be, is assumed to indicate a revolutionary change in the whole nature. By others it is thought that, by some mode of localizing the Divine Presence on earth, the sense of reverence may be deepened, and men be less forgetful of Him. The consecrated wafer in one branch of the Catholic Church, the eucharistic rite in another, with all the attendant ideas (or superstitions, as some would call them) concerning sacred vestments, mystic rites, symbolical worship, and a miracle-working priesthood, are supposed to replace the Temple and the Shechinah of the Jewish Church.

Neither of these methods is in any sense a modern discovery. The latter certainly has had a long trial, and the verdict of history is adverse to its claims. By it you may snatch a temporary victory, but you will have to pay dearly for it. Fighting the demon of infidelity with the broken crutch of superstition in the long run has not succeeded in the past, and is still less likely to do so in the future. History declares that neither method was employed by the most successful missionaries, who also worked under the greatest difficulties—I mean the Apostles and their immediate followers; it declares that growth in morality and in spiritual knowledge have always been in accordance with the laws of continuity and development. Bear, then, these in mind. They are God's laws, and you cannot alter them. First the seed cast upon the earth, then the green blade, then the ear, then the full corn in the ear, and at last, when the fruit is ripe, the season of harvest. Like unto this, we are told by our Master, is the kingdom of God. Therefore be patient. Be content to work along the lines which God has prescribed.

But, you may say, I want to see the fruits of my labours. A very natural feeling. I suppose every one who plants a tree would like to sit under the shadow of it; that, however, is not given to us. But, you may say, this neighbour of mine, by preaching a gospel of hell-fire amidst a blare of trumpets, collects thousands to listen to him; and that neighbour, by the attractions of music, incense, and vestments, gets his church crowded. Well, it is not the making of proselytes, but what we make of them, which matters. For that statement we have pretty good authority. But, you may say, men praise those teachers as earnest and energetic; they will never recognize my work. Recognize your work! what does that matter? The important thing to the world is that the work should be done well, not that it should be recognized. Never mind whether you are praised, whether you may be tracked across the country by newspaper paragraphs: take care that you are not justly blamed: that is the only thing which you need mind. The pulpit of a church is not the stage of a theatre, the sphere of a parson's work is not the area of a circus, and even on these latter he is not the best actor who plays his part to the gallery. Above all, do not make the fatal mistake of supposing that good intentions will render harmless any folly. I sometimes hear it said, So-and-so is such an earnest, zealous, well-meaning man, that we must not criticize or check him. I am sorry to say good intentions will not alter the natural order of events. The best intentions will not save your finger from being burnt if you put it in the fire, and all the zeal in the world will not avert the evil consequences if that zeal is wrongly directed. The words of our great dramatist have a terrible truth—

> "The evil that men do lives after them,
> The good is oft interrèd with their bones."

So long as a man of noble aims but with misdirected energies is acting as leader, that which is hurtful in his system is neutralized by his personal goodness; but when he is gone, and inferior men take his place, the evil part develops and the good withers, because the one is innate and the other adventitious. Antony the hermit and Simeon of the pillar, Francis of Assisi and Ignatius Loyola, not to mention many others among the fathers and doctors of the Church Catholic, were men of the most earnest piety and the very best intentions, but their mistakes have borne and continue to bear a prolific crop of hurtful fruit.

Undertake, then, your work this day in the spirit of patience, in the spirit of self-abnegation, in full trust in God. Let not one word which I have spoken chill your enthusiasm. I only seek to save you from misdirecting it. Never was there a time when there was a grander task before the clergy, or when they could do more to save their country from a great catastrophe. The condition of things in England bears a very dangerous resemblance to that in France before the great Revolution. Not only is there the same widespread poverty, the same unequal distribution of wealth, the same sundering of interests and classes; but there is the same hysteric sentimentality, the same hazy morality, the same confusion of the laws of right and wrong, as there was in that country shortly before the time when men sobbed forth maudlin platitudes about liberty and fraternity, and then went away to torture and murder those who differed from them. It is your business, as was that of the prophets of old, to tell your people in no uncertain voice that God's laws of right and wrong are immutable, and that no amount of verbose oratory or flaccid sentimentality can make a lie into truth, can ennoble a base deed, can change vile tools into honourable implements. It is your business to guide your people to a more perfect sense of the omnipresence, the omnipotence, and the omniscience of the all-loving Father, instead of leading them back towards the worship of idols and the conceptions of times of ignorance. You must be content to work on in silence, for the path which I have described will not be that of earthly fame; in unpopularity, for the prophet's task is a thankless one; in hope, for you will be only a sower of seed. But its fruit will some day ripen; you will not gather it, but others will. In your lifetime, however, you will have this reward, that by degrees you will win the affection and confidence of many, the respect of all whose respect is worth having; and when you cease from labour, you may say—" I have done what I could; it has been little, yet I did it with all my might, and so in God's hands I leave the issue. I have striven, O gracious Saviour, to tread, though at a long distance, in Thy footsteps; to work, though so imperfectly, after Thy example. Failure rather than success has seemed my lot; yet I know that truth is stronger than falsehood, that right will at last prevail over wrong, and in the light of Thy presence all evil will be consumed. The seed which I have sown has borne but little fruit in the brief span of this earthly life, yet I trust to see a more abundant harvest in that better land where the wicked cease from troubling, and the weary are at rest."

THE LILIES OF THE FIELD.[1]

"Consider the lilies of the field, how they grow; they toil not, neither do they spin: and yet I say unto you, That even Solomon in all his glory was not arrayed like one of these."—
ST. MATT. VI. 28, 29.

LIFE had its anxieties nineteen centuries since no less than it has now; men and women had to toil for food and for clothing, and sometimes knew not whence to-morrow's bread would come. But then, even as now, they were apt to weary themselves by seeking more than a sufficiency; to deprive life of all its light, in order that they might heap up riches, might fare sumptuously every day, and go clothed in purple and fine linen. Here, then, we are told on Whom to cast our care in those anxieties which may be called lawful, and the unwisdom of those which are unlawful; we are led to see the Fatherhood of God in the fowls of the air and in the flowers of the field.

But on the general principle inculcated by this

[1] The "Fairchild Lecture," preached in Shoreditch Church, Whitsun Tuesday, 1890.

reference, I do not now purpose to speak. I shall restrict myself to a few thoughts which seem appropriate to the present occasion, and arise out of the example selected by the Saviour to show the unwisdom of anxious thought for this world's wealth.

"Consider the lilies of the field." What flowers were they, we naturally ask, from which the listeners were to take a lesson? Were they conspicuous for their beauty? Did they rise high above the general level, like the butterfly-orchis or the purple loosestrife; or were they common but inconspicuous, like the daisy of our lawns, or the celandine of our meadows? Was the appeal to something which the hearers could hardly help admiring, or to something which they might almost despise? Was it as though the Saviour had said, "You cannot rival the beauty of the orchid;" or was it, "Adorn yourselves as you will, you are still far less fair than the daisy, insignificant as it may seem in your eyes"? Either sense is possible, and we have no means of knowing which is intended. But it is more probable, I think, that the appeal was made to some flowers which, at any rate, were conspicuous enough to catch the eyes of those who were listening—flowers which at that very time were dappling the slopes in view of the hill on which the crowd was gathered. There are many such in

S

Palestine. They are called lilies in our Bible. This is the English name by which the original Greek word is always rendered, but of course we cannot assert that the terms in the two languages are exactly identical. The Greek word probably would be employed more generally and vaguely than the English one; it might include some plants which we should not designate as lilies, and we must remember that it is only a translation of the actual word which was used by our Lord, for we cannot doubt that He was speaking in the ordinary language of the country—a dialect of Hebrew. We should naturally, I think, look for such a flower as our daffodil or primrose; one which was common in Galilee, which was sufficiently large to be seen at some distance, and which was attractive in appearance. Of these, travellers tell us, there are several. Bulbous plants abound on the hilly pastures of Northern Palestine in the springtime—such as the tulip, the fritillary, the star of Bethlehem, the iris, and the amaryllis. There is also, in Galilee, a scarlet anemone, of which it is said by one traveller, well competent to express an opinion, "There have been many claimants for the distinctive honour of 'the lilies of the field;' but while it seems most natural to view the term as a generic expression, yet if one special flower was more likely than another to catch the eye of the Lord as He spoke, no one familiar with the flora of Palestine in springtime can hesitate in assigning the place to the anemone."[1]

Yet this flower of the field, whatever it may have been, is declared to surpass in beauty " Solomon in all his glory." Think for one moment of the comparison which is here challenged. We must remember the customs of past times and of Eastern nations in order to appreciate it fully. Among ourselves there is usually little splendour of dress to mark rank and even royalty. In olden time, and in the East, it was not so. That a king would appear in public so clothed as to be with difficulty distinguished from one of his ministers, or one of his generals, would have seemed a strange idea. Then splendour of apparel went with high rank, and "Solomon in all his glory" would mean at least as much as the " Queen in her coronation robes" would now signify. More than this, the reign of Solomon, in popular tradition, was the golden age of Israel. It was literally so; the shields of his household guards, the ornaments of his ivory throne, the plate at his table, were all of gold. " Gold came to him in abundance ; as for silver, it was not anything accounted of in the days of Solomon." Yet the glory of the central figure in all this splendour—a splendour

[1] Canon Tristram, *Land of Israel*, ch. xviii.

which overpowered the spirit of the Queen of Sheba —is said to be surpassed by the flower which in each returning spring blossoms in its uncounted thousands on the hill-pastures around the Galilæan lake.

It is true; and after more than eighteen centuries of progress we know its truth, far better than those who heard, perhaps half incredulously, the words of Christ. God's work may be tried by a standard which man's work cannot bear. This is made for the eyes of man. The work of God can endure a far more severe test, as though it were designed for powers of intelligence far more perfect. The perfection of the one is only relative; of the other, so far as we know, absolute of its kind. Familiar as the facts may be to some of you, it is, I think, worth while to contrast, for a few minutes, man's works of art and God's works in nature. To take a single example. I have seen the image of a small sewing-needle, greatly magnified, projected upon a screen. You would think that if anything would be sharp and smooth and finished, it would be the point of this. I saw the outline of a small mast, with its upper end trimmed to a rough spike, which terminated in a rather jagged tooth or wisp of metal. Far different is it with the structures of plant or of animal. The more these are magnified, the more marvellous, the more exquisite, they appear.

That this is simple truth, most people, at the present day, can sometimes ascertain for themselves, but there is one test which can be yet more readily applied. A fairly good pocket-lens is generally not difficult to obtain. Look through this at a few of the commonest wayside flowers. Pick, if you like, a daisy from the nearest plot of grass on which you may walk. To your eye it seems one of the homeliest of flowers— a little circular cluster of yellow dots with a fringe of white petals just edged with pink. If these were made of the finest tissues of the loom, if they were painted by the hand of the most cunning artist, they would seem, when largely magnified, coarse fabrics like sackcloth, coarsely spotted with colour. Not so the petal of the daisy; its texture becomes yet more exquisite; its coloured edge breaks up into granulations yet more and more delicate in tint and in size, rendering the transition yet more and more harmonious. Turn then to those spots on the yellow disc; each becomes a perfect little flower, revealing many a complicated detail, of the existence of which you previously had no conception.

Man often boasts of the wonders which he has done. Comparing himself with himself, the civilized man with the savage; looking at the complicated apparatus which he has contrived—his machines, his railroads, his telegraphs,—he begins to think that to his greatness there is no limit, and that he may worship himself as God. Can there be any rebuke more gentle, yet more crushing, than this: "The common wayside flowers, at which you scarce cast a glance, which even your sheep and oxen trample underfoot,—these are far more wonderful than all your contrivances, far more exquisitely finished than any of your works. Poor vain insect! for in comparison with this vast universe you are nothing more; there is but one thing wonderful about you— that which you do not make yourself—your own body"!

Another lesson may be drawn from this saying of the Saviour. Here, as on more than one occasion, He appeals in His teaching to the natural world. But some persons tell us that this is everywhere tainted with sin; nay, they go so far as to hint that it is so corrupt that the very study of nature will lead us away from God. They assert, not indeed expressly, but in so many words, that if in truth God were the Maker of this world—as they are obliged to admit—He allowed it at a very early period to be wrested from His dominion by an alien and an evil power. It would not be difficult, but it would take too long a time, to show that this idea—a very common one among Christian people—arises from confused thinking and mistaken conceptions as to the nature of sin and evil; on the present occasion it will suffice to say that Christ's frequent appeal to the natural world could not have been made if it had ceased to be a part of the kingdom of God. If, indeed, the devil has become lord of any spot on earth, it is not where the lilies of the field mostly do grow, or the birds of the air make their nests, but it is where the buildings reared by man stand thickest on the ground. We talk sometimes of consecrating places to God's service, but except as a precautionary measure to save them from man's desecration, or a symbolical cleansing from man's defilement, the ceremony is idle and meaningless. The earth itself is consecrated; it is a sacred thing, for it is as it came from God's hand. The lilies of the field, if they toil not, neither do they spin, so also they spoil not, neither do they sin. Men sometimes profess to hear the voice of God in the thunder and the tempest, but they are too often deaf to that still small voice which sounds in Nature's most silent hour, alike from tree and flower, from forest and from field.

There is another way in which these words suggest a lesson of humility. Man is sent to learn from the commonest and least esteemed among the works of

God; not from the choice flowers of the garden, but from those which spring up unheeded in every pasture. We talk sometimes as if this world were made for us alone. If so, there is a strange profusion, almost a wastefulness, in the provision for us, its lords and masters. Year after year the earth puts on its robe of many colours, yet how few regard it! There are vast forests, where for century after century, generation after generation, the giant trees have grown and died; there are wide plains, there are broad chains of rolling hills, which year after year have been gardens of flowers on which the eye of man has never looked. Even among the mountain solitudes, amid regions of snow and ice, when we reach some crag on which hitherto the foot of man has never been set, we find the crannies among the rough rocks bright with the blossoms of some lowly but lovely alpine plant. Nay, the earth was decked in all the glory of flowers for myriad years or ever it was seen by the eye of man. Were these, are these, for him alone? It may be so, and doubtless the idea is flattering to our complacency; but on what grounds do we make this assumption? Why may there not be those who see with clearer eyes than ours? Why must we suppose that the shout of joy which the sons of God are said to have raised over the completion of the work of creation has died away into an eternal silence, in watching the never-ending recurrence of its effects, and the manifestations of the Will of God?

"Love not the world," we are told; but the words mean the order of man's contriving, not that of God's ordaining. In the old creation story it is said that God planted a garden, wherein He placed the man and the woman. Like all the rest of that story, this seems to me symbolical. Face to face with the works of God, there was the fitting abode of innocence; there communion with Him could best be held. Of this parable we have lost sight. We have come to associate the worship of Him with buildings made with hands, forgetting that the Lord is in every place, and not least in those which are of His own adorning. The houses which we build are apt to become temples of idols, when we forget that after all they are only concessions to man's infirmity; for God may be found, as He was by the saints of old, on any country-side, where man can possess his soul in silence and listen for that still small voice, which may be heard to whisper from every green slope no less than among the wild crags of Horeb. We need to be reminded of this, for year by year in our densely crowded land, with the gorged but ever-growing towns, it becomes more difficult to consider the lilies of the field. No longer is the country-side within easy reach of the Londoner; it is a journey of miles before he can get clear of the houses, and, what is worse, the edge of a great town is more hideous than the inner part. Far beyond its border, almost every spot is fenced or walled or barred, because men fear the inroads of those brutes in human form, which a great city is constantly vomiting forth for the destruction of all that is fair and beautiful. For miles around London every wild flower is disappearing—destroyed either of reckless selfishness, or of sheer wantonness, by the excursionist or by those prowling plunderers, who bring back the uprooted plants, and obtain as public nuisances a miserable living. They are half protected in their errands of destruction by the flabby sentimentalism of the present day, which is ever ready to sympathize with the breaker, and to blame the enforcer of the law. They are encouraged by the thoughtlessness which enables them to find a sale for their spoil, for if there were no purchasers the wild flowers would be left to grow. If the destruction of these goes on for another generation as it has done in the last, your children or grandchildren will have to content themselves with considering the lilies of the gardens or of the parks, for there will be nothing left for them in the fields except nettles and docks.

But I must admit that sometimes those who should know better set an example of evil influence. There is a practice in some countries—and an attempt, I believe, has been made to naturalize it in this—of holding what is called a battle of flowers. This means that in idle sport these gifts of God are flung about recklessly, are prevented from fulfilling their course and ripening seed to perpetuate their kind, plucked not that they may gladden the eyes and brighten the dulness of those who dwell in the stony wilderness of a great city, but that they may move children of larger growth to a foolish mirth, and then be trampled underfoot like worthless and contemptible things. There is something tender, something touching, in the sentiment exhibited by the flower-services sometimes held at this season, even though they are apt to lead to a waste of flowers; but those who fling the same about merely for destruction, put wealth to an ill purpose, and show the heart of the savage beneath all their purple and fine linen.

To some what I have been saying may seem poetic sentiment and fruitless fancy. It is, I believe, real and important truth. Faulty religious teaching, mistaken theological ideas, have closed the eyes of numbers of men and women to that great book of nature, the pages of which are daily turned, the volumes of which are yearly renewed by the power of God. The book of the revelation of the written Word is great, it is inestimably precious; but why on this account should we refuse to listen to that other voice, which is no less the voice of God? We pride ourselves upon our wisdom, yet we have forgotten truths which were well known by the men of olden time. The Jew found himself, in his fields and his vineyards, his sheep-downs and forests, face to face with God; the earlier Christians sought the wilderness when they would find Him. The Bible again and again takes up the note of thanksgiving for the works of God. We also, if we would purge ourselves from the worship of idols—be they set up in things spiritual or things temporal—must submit to go back to the simple teaching of the Sermon on the Mount, and learn from the lilies of the field and the fowls of the air the great lesson of the Fatherhood of God; for when that is realized in our hearts and lives, all other things shall be added to it.

THE ORIGIN OF EVIL.[1]

WHENCE came evil; what was its origin? This is an old question, for it is more easy to ask than to answer. It is a difficulty which cannot fail to arise, so soon as man has become conscious of moral responsibility and has recognized God as Creator and Lord of all things. Thus any discussion might seem idle, for by this time the problem should have been either solved or admitted to be inscrutable. But in the past it has been regarded mainly from the point of view of the metaphysician or the theologian; the advance of knowledge during late years has introduced new factors into the discussion. We have learnt much concerning the past history of the earth and our own race; our knowledge of the relation between the physical, mental, and moral natures in ourselves has vastly increased. New facts have risen up on our horizon, of which we must take account

[1] The substance of a paper read at Sion College on February 24, 1890, delivered as an afternoon lecture at St. Philip's, Regent Street, on the Fifth Sunday in Lent.

in framing any hypothesis in regard to man and his motives. In short, whether we like it or not, distrustful as we may feel of the new-comer, doubtful whether it be friend or foe, we are compelled to adopt methods of inquiry which are more strictly scientific. Thus, while we are beginning to recognize more clearly that the provinces of theology and science are distinct, that we must not look to the former to teach us the latter, or fear that the latter can be in essential contradiction with the former, we now prefer facts to phrases, and inductions to authorities.

I purpose, then, in the remarks which I am about to make, to abstain from investigating the past history of the subject. I shall not quote what has been written by others, or attempt to discuss the problem from a point of view strictly metaphysical; nor shall I, except indirectly, regard it from that of theology, or seek to solve a difficulty by quotations, either from a Father of the Church or from Scripture itself. The latter undoubtedly have their place and their value, but there is sometimes a distinct gain in regarding a difficult subject from a new point of view. Let us, then, try to look at it from that of a student of science, to whom the book of nature is more familiar than the volumes of theologians, who dares hope to find in it some light which may illuminate dark sayings even in the Word of God.

We assume, indeed—and this, no doubt, is a theological position—that God is the Author of all things, and that He is perfect goodness. If, then, this be accepted—as it must be by all Christians—what account is to be given of the origin of evil? The inquiry, however, at once suggests a preliminary question, an answer to which is imperatively demanded, namely, What do we mean by the word "evil"? This is commonly assumed to be as definite in its meaning as a mathematical term; yet in reality, to most of us, its position in our verbal exchange is not unlike that which a Chinese silver coin would occupy in a business transaction. We should have a rough notion, but no precise idea of its value in currency. Thus we can hardly listen to an argument or take up a book without detecting traces of confusion in thought and vagueness in expression which are due to this uncertainty. Indeed, in common speech the word "evil" is used to connote two ideas widely distinct, different, as I believe, in their inception, even though they become entangled and sometimes almost inseparable in the complicated nature and history of man.

Physical and moral evil—to use the ordinary qualifying terms, and admit for the moment the double sense of the noun—are commonly supposed to be similar in nature, and, so far as this world is concerned, identical in origin. Many persons, I believe, would tell you that both were the consequence of the fall of man (of which phrase I do not at present discuss the meaning). There is in the tenth book of the *Paradise Lost* a well-known passage, from which I will select some extracts:—

> "At that tasted fruit
> The sun, as from Thyéstean banquet, turned
> His course intended. . . . Thus began
> Outrage from lifeless things; but Discord first,
> Daughter of Sin, among the irrational
> Death introduced, through fierce antipathy.
> Beast now with beast 'gan war, and fowl with fowl,
> And fish with fish: to graze the herb all leaving,
> Devoured each other."

These words, I think, give a very fair summary of the view which is held generally by the uneducated, and not very seldom even by theologians.

Now, what can we learn from science as to the date of the incoming of pain, disease, and death to this earth? The general tenor of the answer, if we attach any value to inductive processes and results, is beyond dispute.

Thus Science replies: The crust of the earth is a great charnel-house. Death hath reigned on it from the beginning. Predaceous animals date from an early—perhaps a very early—period in its history, and even the herbivorous cannot have moved about or fed without being the cause of injury or death to those smaller and weaker than themselves. We are fully justified in maintaining that the earth, even before life began, was subject to physical forces—such as gravitation, heat, electricity—identical with those which still operate. Hence, unless we suppose that organized beings were endowed with properties of which we have no knowledge, and, things being as they are, can form no conception, they could not escape from the pain and suffering to which they are at present exposed in their natural state of life.

Suppose, however, that to the statement, "Death reigned from the beginning," it were answered, "Yes, but death may have been painless—even pleasurable, like falling asleep?" But is it possible for an animal capable of sensation to receive an injury without the consequent pain? Indeed, it is difficult to conceive of the capacity for a pleasurable sensation existing in beings constituted as those of which we know, without admitting a capacity for the contrary sensation; there can be little or no doubt that, as a rule, each is perceived with corresponding acuteness. Moreover, pain in many cases results from either the absence or the excess of that which is pleasurable. For instance, a certain temperature produces in myself, but not necessarily in another person, the sensation of pleasure. Less than this or more than this would cause in me, and might cause in both, a sensation of pain.

Further, in many cases pain is either protective in its effects—as when it serves to warn us of danger—or a stimulus to exertion. If, then, we suppose the world to have been subject in the past to the laws which now exist, pain and pleasure are inseparable from its order; indeed, have been the dominant factors in its evolution, as they must be in every system of education. Pain is as inseparable from pleasure, as shadow from light, cold from heat. Under the existing order of things there is a necessary dualism, though it is not that of the Manichee. So, if we use the word "evil" in its physical sense, as meaning sickness, pain, and death, we have no choice but to admit that these are inseparable from the present order of nature, and must have entered into its original design, whatever form of teleology we may adopt.

Let us pass on to consider moral evil, which is generally meant when the word "evil" is used in its stricter sense. How came this into the world; what was its beginning? If we regard God as the Creator of all things, are we not driven to regard Him as the

Author of evil; and if so, what follows? So far as this world is concerned, people have been content generally to regard evil as an importation from without—though this, of course, only shifts the main difficulty rather further back. But can we predicate an independency of origin and absoluteness of existence for moral evil? Are we right in assuming it, as so many appear to do, to be a positive? Antagonistic as it may be to good, is it not, under the existing order, correlative to some extent with it? They are opposites, it is true, because a thing cannot be at once sweet and sour; but correlative, and in thought inseparable, because a necessary consequence of heterogeneity. Ought we not, then, to regard evil, at any rate in its inception, whatever complications may afterwards arise, as a relative?—much as, in the physical order, darkness is relative to light? Light is a positive; it is a mode of motion. Darkness is a negative—a non-existent; no motion. Our perception of it also is relative, dependent on the environment of the perceiver. It is dark to me when it is not so to a bat or an owl, and they are blinded with excess of light when I can see distinctly.

Perhaps we may arrive at a clearer understanding by tracing out in a particular instance the development of our idea of evil. Hunger, to any organized being, is the stimulus to obtain food, which is needful for the maintenance of life. Suppose that I leave my food for a time unprotected in some desert place. A hungry wild dog passes by and snaps it up. We *say* the dog steals it, but I think no one would seriously affirm that the animal had done evil. I might, indeed, kill it, but should do this on the principle that there was not room for both of us in the world, and so I, as the stronger and, in my own opinion, the more important of the two, elected to be the survivor. My own dog, in like case, I should chastise; the punishment, however, would not have a moral aim—though, being inflicted for educational purposes, it would come near this—but its intent would be to procure for myself a security from future loss, which in the other case I knew could not be obtained by a mild remedy. If a very young child were the thief, we should view the action in precisely the same light. Having an eye to the future, we should indicate displeasure; but we should not regard the action as a crime, because, as we say, "he knows no better." But if the child were older, we should say he had done wrong, because we suppose him to have acquired some idea that it is better to suffer than to steal; yet even here we should estimate his guilt in accordance with the extent of his need and the defect of his education.

If, however, a well-fed and well-taught child were to steal simply for the sake of a dainty morsel, we should regard the action as a grave moral wrong, and requite it accordingly.

Here, then, the act is one and the same; yet in its moral aspect it is very differently regarded; namely, from not evil at all, to being very evil.

Apply the same method of examination to all sorts of wrongs and crimes, and you will find that you can trace them back to an obedience to some impulse or instinct which operates in the animal either for the preservation of the individual or for the perpetuation of the race.

At first sight this statement may seem questionable, but I believe that on investigation it will be found to hold good. Murder, for example, is the misuse of instincts the end of which is self-preservation; lust, the abuse of sensations which lead to the perpetuation of the species. Even a crime like forgery, the illegitimate offspring, as we think it, of civilization, is prompted by the desire to obtain the means of living or of enjoyment, a desire which is the outcome of instincts of self-preservation. Very often the right or wrong in an action is entirely determined by the motive of the doer, and we admit tacitly that evil, if it exist, is relative rather than absolute. For instance, there are cases in which most persons, perhaps all, will admit that killing is no murder, or is even a righteous act.

What, then, causes the difference in the moral value of actions in themselves identical? Evidently it is the impulse which has been obeyed in doing it. But why do we view this in different lights in different individuals? Because we tacitly and implicitly assume that two impulses have contended for mastery in the one person, and that the lower of these has been obeyed. As "lower" and "higher" are relative terms, and as we have no right (at any rate, as Christians), when there is but one impulse, to speak of this as evil in itself—for that would be taking up the position of a Manichæan—it would appear that the idea of choice in beings constituted as we are involves, by implication, that of evil, because in speaking of "choice" we assume the existence of a relatively better and worse. A physical illustration may serve to bring out my meaning. Suppose that, wittingly and without good reason, I take that which I know to be the less beneficial to me—say I eat something which I am convinced is unwholesome. I have obeyed the law of self-preservation in its letter and not in its spirit; that is to say, by yielding to an appetite (the end of which is self-preservation), I have injured my health, and thus produced an opposite result. I have chosen to follow the narrower view of the law, and thus I have done evil, while one who had acted in ignorance would still be innocent, though the physical penalties in both cases would be the same.

Extend the application of this principle, and it follows that a course of action may be right at one period of the world's history which is wrong at another. For instance, at a particular epoch it might have been right to punish one who had wronged us, but in the present age, when wider views of man's nature and his relationships have prevailed, it may be better, under the same circumstances, to pardon him. The line of action which once would have been right now would be wrong, because we, knowing both the lower and the higher law, choose to obey the former.

It follows, then, that if, in beings organized as we are, we assume a power of choice and the existence of impulses tending to progress, we must admit the possibility of a refusal to obey those impulses, and thus regard evil as the inevitable shadow of the good. Thus any creatures which are living in perfect harmony with their environment (using that word in its widest sense) are good, but the alteration of the environment, if it tend to raise them to a higher plane of existence, supposing them to be free agents, would open to them the opportunity of becoming evil. Formerly their moral equilibrium would have been stable. The alteration of the conditions has rendered this unstable, and they become capable of evil.

Let us now consider how evil may have first arisen in the case of man. So far as regards his physical structure, it is impossible to separate him from other living creatures. Such differences as there may be are those of degree, not of kind. So far as his body is concerned, there is nothing to suggest an origin for it different from that of their bodies. We cannot, of course, deny that it may result from a special act of creation; but analogy, so far from favouring, is rather adverse to this idea.

All attempts to establish a difference in kind between the bodily frame of man and that of animals have been complete failures. I cannot say that the efforts to claim for him the sole possession of reason have been more successful. If the true man differs, as I believe that he does differ, from the rest of the animal world, it is by the addition of something which we hold to be the special gift of God—that by which he becomes capable of attaining to the knowledge of God and to an immortal life. The presence of this gift in man can neither be proved nor be disproved by science. Our investigations bring us no further than this—that there are phenomena in the world very difficult to explain on a merely mechanical theory of the genesis of the universe, and facts in history which seem inexplicable on the hypothesis that man is no more than an animal. Suppose, now, that man's body, instead of being the result, as has generally been believed, of a special act of creation, had arisen, by gradual and progressive stages of development, from less perfectly organized animal forms, in obedience to that great law of evolution which seems to have been prevalent in this world since the dawn of life. Suppose, in short, that the body of man were in its origin truly animal—inheritor of the same instincts, animated by the same vitality. Suppose, then, that in such a creature were implanted an impulse—call it what you will—to live no longer in obedience to the instincts which actuated the remainder of the animal world, to follow a path which had been trodden by no predecessor, to commence the ascent of a mountain range, the summit of which was lost in the clouds, instead of roaming contentedly over the plains below. Such a being would at once become capable of evil. Conceive such a one placed in a position which gave some special advantage to the new impulse, and tended to deaden the inherited instincts when they might mislead.

Such a creature would be sinless in nature, because its inherited tendencies would be those of obedience to law, for up to that time it had never been invited to disobey. It would be the first of a new race, with responsibilities which were unknown to any predecessor. But it would not follow that these were as far-reaching and as complicated as those which have affected the successors of that creature. It is enough that there was an opportunity of choice between obedience to the higher law (whether prohibitive or directive), and following the course suggested by the animal instincts. The moral nature of such a creature, though for a time it be sinless, is obviously in unstable equilibrium; and, we may add, is likely, when once the disturbance occurs, to depart further from its original condition.

The equilibrium was maintained so long as the instinct, which might ultimately disturb it, was dormant—very much as in the individual, for a time, certain kinds of evil, though always potentially present, are excluded by the undeveloped condition of certain organs in the body. But after a disturbance of equilibrium, the effect of heredity would be unfavourable to recovery, because the innate instincts of conformity to the environment, which is no longer in the old relation to the individual and the race, may work in the wrong direction, and cause as vigorous a resistance to the upward tendency as it should have done to the downward. The balance of such a nature once disturbed, it is thrown into a confusion from which it can never emerge by any natural process. The slow effect of environment may result in the high development of these tendencies, and the partial abortion of those; but even then there will be individual irregularity—" throwings back," as they are called, which will interfere with anything like a perfect symmetry. Moreover, it is not probable that by merely natural processes any very perfect moral development will be attained, because the environment favours the development of the animal far more than of the spiritual nature. The latter bases its claim to obedience on things of which the senses cannot take cognizance; but hunger, thirst, cold, nakedness, are often grim realities. The pleasures derived from the gratification of the bodily appetites are real, they may be said to have an objective existence; while those resulting from the due exercise of the spiritual appetites, at any rate to a great extent, are subjective.

If, then, we feel ourselves compelled by the results of scientific investigations to admit for the body of man the same origin as for those of animals, we are placed in a position which enables us to offer a simple explanation of the origin of evil. The mere animal, in harmony with its environment, was good in its generation. But by the addition to it of that mysterious gift, commonly called a soul, evil became at once possible, because then that which had been good, viz. obedience to the earlier laws, now became evil, as involving a disobedience to the newer and higher laws. The principle of heredity, to use a scientific term, indicates that "the infection of nature must remain even in the regenerate," for the simple reason that it was always there, only it did not become an "infection" till some particular epoch, and it cannot disappear so long as this bodily frame continues.

Before I conclude, it may be well to notice an objection which some have felt. It may be briefly expressed thus: that by tracing evil to an obedience on the part of man to his physical nature, we interfere with the due appreciation of moral responsibility. How can you, it is said, hold a man morally responsible for obedience to a propensity which you assert to be innate, and thus to be a part of the man himself, as much as a tendency to scrofula or other maladies? Of this objection I cannot see the force. Society, which punishes crime chiefly with a deterrent purpose, recognizes in certain extreme cases that the individual is not responsible, and that the legal penalty ought not to be inflicted. As, for example, when an insane person commits a murder, he is not executed, but is kept under ward for the security of the public. There may, then, be cases where the commission of sin, as we call it, entails no guilt, because the offender is morally insane. But in regard to this we have no means available for forming a judgment: that must be left to Him Who sees with larger eyes than ours. With such questions we can only deal as society does with crime, namely, by acting on the facts within our cognizance; and we cannot even make the same exceptions, because we have no criteria of moral insanity. Of course, if we asserted that man was no more than an animal, we should admit that he was not morally responsible for his actions; but when we affirm that in his composite nature a factor exists, which urges him to resist the others and submit wholly to its guidance, then we assert the existence of moral responsibility. In this inquiry we have only endeavoured to throw some light on the sources which give rise to temptation and eventuate in sin.

The remarks which I have made apply only to the world of which we have cognizance by means of our senses. Here I have endeavoured to distinguish between what is termed physical evil—viz. pain, suffering, and those things which are misfortunes inseparable from the present order—and moral evil, to indicate how under changed environment conflict may replace harmony, and ultimate good be the cause of temporary ill.

The limitations which I imposed upon my inquiry, namely, to consider it from the side of science rather than of revelation, have prevented me from saying anything about the existence of evil among orders of beings other than human, and of their possible influence upon members of our race; but it is obvious that a similar line of reasoning would explain its presence among beings of any kind in any part of God's universe, for there is no reason why this command to rise "on stepping-stones of their dead selves to higher things" should be restricted to mankind.

THE END.

www.ingramcontent.com/pod-product-compliance
Lightning Source LLC
Chambersburg PA
CBHW031906220426
43663CB00006B/788